PEOPLE IN HISTORY

PEOPLE IN HISTORY

ARTISTS HOUSE

Researched and Compiled by: Martin Folly
Executive Managers: Kelly Flynn, Susan Egerton-Jones
Editor: Avril Price-Budgen
Art Editor: Hans Verkroost
Picture Research: Pat Hodgson
Production: Peter Phillips, Barbara Hind

Mitchell Beazley International Ltd
Michelin House
81 Fulham Road
London
SW3 6RB

"An Artists House Book"
© Mitchell Beazley International Ltd 1988
Reprinted 1991, 1993

ISBN 0 86134 114 7

Typeset by Hourds Typographica, Stafford
Reproduction by La Cromolito s.n.c., Milan
Produced by Mandarin Offset
Printed in Malaysia

CONTENTS

INTRODUCTION

At the heart of all the turning points of history are people. Whether individuals, specific groups or nations, the great figures of history arise sometimes from a chance single development or from broader changes affecting society. These people have added a significant contribution to the shape of the world as we know it today. Coming from backgrounds of religion, politics or science, the strength of their beliefs, philosophies or inventiveness has moulded societies through the centuries. History is a living subject; some people alive today will become great figures of history tomorrow.

The shape of the religious world owes much to men such as Abraham, Pope Gregory and John Wesley, to name but three. Behind revolutions are such names as Oliver Cromwell, Thomas Paine and Robespierre. Industry pushed ahead through the endeavours of people like Richard Arkwright and James Watt, while communications opened up the world with the help of George Stephenson, Henry Ford and Marconi. From leaders in wartime – Winston Churchill and Charles de Gaulle – to leaders in peaceful change such as Mahatma Gandhi and Martin Luther King, each historical figure marks a point at which the world took an irrevocable step into the future. Some have been made infamous by their deeds such as Hitler and Mussolini; on the other hand we find a stark contrast in the commitment of Darwin and Florence Nightingale who strove to expand the knowledge and conditions of mankind respectively.

In *People in History* we have selected a few of the most famous people who have given shape to life today. There are many names missing, but those whose histories we briefly discuss here have been included because we believe they are broadly representative of all the major twists and turns in world history.

Abraham

c.2000 BC

Abraham is revered as the father of the Hebrew nation. The first book of the Bible, Genesis, tells how he settled in Palestine, the Biblical homeland of the Jews. As well as being an important Jewish figure he also occupies an important place in Christian teachings as a man of unquestioning faith.

Abraham originally lived in the land of the Chaldees, in the city of Ur, at the junction of the great Tigris and Euphrates rivers, in what is today Iraq. He was then known as Abram (which means "the Father is exalted"). He left Ur at the age of 75, with his wife Sarai and his nephew Lot, and journeyed for many months through modern-day Iraq, Turkey and Syria, until they came to Hebron (now in Southern Israel). Abram's people were traditionally nomads, travelling with their flocks of sheep and other animals, from pasture to pasture. However, these wanderings of Abram's were done with greater purpose, for Abram believed he was commanded by God to leave Ur and establish a new homeland for his descendants, although he was old and childless. He adopted the name Abraham, "the father of many nations", and his wife became Sarah, "princess".

For many years, Abraham was without a child, and as Sarah was now old, he turned to his wife's servant, Hagar, who bore him a son Ishmael. However, Sarah, who had despaired of ever having a child, had her prayers answered, and Isaac was born.

In order to test Abraham's faith, God commanded Abraham to take Isaac away to a mountain-top, and kill him as a sacrifice. Though saddened by his task, Abraham took the boy with him to Mount Moriah, and bound him and prepared to kill him. Satisfied that Abraham was prepared to obey, even to the extent of losing his beloved son, God commanded him at the last moment to take a ram caught by its horns in a nearby gorse bush, and sacrifice that instead.

Abraham lived to be 175 years old, according to the Bible, and when he died was buried in the cave that had been the first piece of land he had bought on arrival in the "Promised Land". Through Isaac and his son Israel, who had twelve sons of his own, Abraham's descendants peopled the land, and formed the Jewish race, as Abraham had been promised way back in the land of the Chaldees.

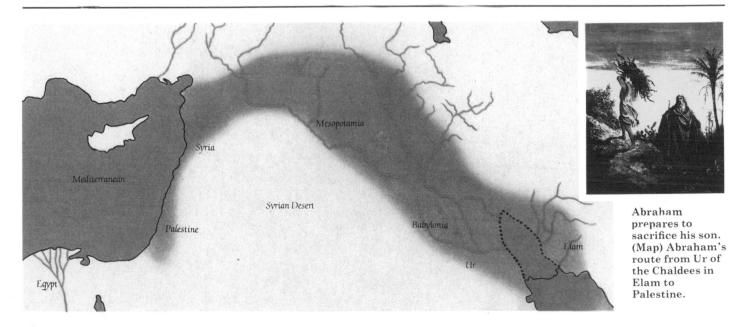

Abraham prepares to sacrifice his son. (Map) Abraham's route from Ur of the Chaldees in Elam to Palestine.

Moses
late 13th Century BC

Moses was the great law-giver of the Jewish nation whose moral code is at the heart of Jewish and Christian teachings.

Moses was born in Egypt, where the Jews lived in subjection to the Egyptians. As a baby, he was hidden by his mother in bullrushes on the bank of the River Nile, to hide him from Pharoah's men, who had orders to kill all new-born Jewish boys. He was discovered by Pharoah's daughter, who adopted him as her own. Moses grew up as a prince in Egypt, but had to flee the country when he killed an Egyptian who was beating a Jew. One day, while in exile, Moses saw a bush, burning without being consumed by flames. Out of the bush he heard the voice of God, commanding him to return to Egypt, and lead his people out of captivity, into a "land of milk and honey". When Moses protested his unworthiness for such task, God gave him a staff, which could turn into a snake.

Moses did return, and with his brother Aaron, tried to get Pharoah to allow the Jews to leave. He would not do so until God had inflicted ten plagues on the Egyptians. The last plague involved the death of all the first-born sons of Egypt, and in order to be spared, the Jews marked their doorposts with lamb's blood, so that the angel of death passed over. Jews still celebrate the "Passover" as their major festival of the year.

Although Pharoah now allowed them to go, he followed them with his soldiers. When they reached the Red Sea, the Jews thought they were trapped, but Moses raised his staff, and the seas were parted, and the Jews passed through. When Pharoah attempted to follow, the waters rushed in and his chariots, horses and men were swept away.

The Jews journeyed for 40 years in the wilderness. When they reached Mount Sinai, it was surrounded by clouds and thunder. Moses went to the top, and returned with two tablets of stone, bearing the Ten Commandments. Moses died before the Jews reached the Promised Land, but the laws he laid down, contained in the Biblical books Exodus, Leviticus, Deuteronomy and Numbers, became the basis of the code of behaviour of the Jews (the *Torah*). The Ten Commandments have had a great influence not only on the Jews, but on mankind as a whole. Moses was a courageous, but humble leader, who is regarded by the Jews as second only to Abraham, and did much to transform his people from wandering shepherds into a nation.

(Right) The boy Moses is presented to Pharoah's daughter.

King David

reigned c.1000 BC–962 BC

David established a dynasty that ruled the Jewish kingdoms of Judah and Israel for 40 years. He started the building of the Great Temple in Jerusalem and wrote at least some of the psalms in the Bible. He was regarded in later years as the ideal king, and many hoped for him to come again, as the "messiah" or saviour of the Jews.

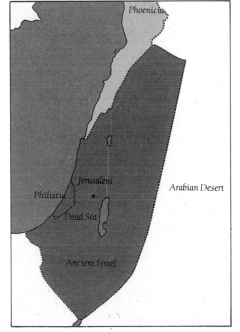

David was a shepherd's son, whose abilities at playing the harp won him the favour of King Saul, for David's playing was the only thing that would ease Saul's troubled mind. He won universal popularity, when, armed only with his shepherd's slingshot and five smooth pebbles he defeated and killed the Philistine giant Goliath, from whom all the great warriors of Israel had fled.

David made close friends with Saul's son Jonathan, and married his daughter, Michal. He attracted Saul's jealousy, and was forced to live like Robin Hood as an outlaw in caves on the edges of the kingdom. He remained loyal, however, and on the deaths of Saul and Jonathan, he was asked to become king, first of Judah, then of Israel.

As king, he united the two kingdoms, and extended their lordship over neighbouring territories, including the city of Jerusalem. He did this partly by conquest and partly by alliances based on his marriage to daughters of the ruler.

David had many wives, one of whom, Bathsheba, he acquired by underhand methods. Bathsheba was married to Uriah, a Hittite, and David ordered his army commander to place Uriah in the place of greatest danger in a battle. Uriah was killed, as David planned, and he duly married Bathsheba.

It was not clear which of his wives' children would succeed him, and one of them, Absalom, attempted to stake his claim early. He was nearly successful, and actually drove David out of Jerusalem for a time, but was finally killed, which David deeply regretted. David was succeeded by his son by Bathsheba, Solomon, who completed the work of building the great Temple in Jerusalem, begun by David, which from that time has been the Holy City of the Jewish faith.

(Far left) David has inspired many works of art. A detail of the most famous is shown here, Michelangelo's larger than life statue in Florence, Italy.
(Map) The empire of David and his son Solomon. David united the ancient kingdoms of Judah and Israel, and added to their territories by conquest.
(Left) After David had killed Goliath with his slingshot, he cut off his head with the giant's own sword, and showed it in triumph to the Israelite army. The demoralized Philistines were rapidly defeated.

Cyrus the Great

c.600–529 BC

Cyrus II of Persia, known as the Great, was the founder of the first great empire in known history. He was held in high esteem by the Ancient Greeks, many of whose writers cited him as an example of the wise ruler. The Iranians (as Persians are now called) regard him as the father of their country.

Cyrus' birth and early life is surrounded by legend. It was said that Cyrus' grandfather, the King of the Medes, dreamed that Cyrus would overthrow him, and ordered the baby to be killed. His chief adviser could not bring himself to do this and instead gave the child to a shepherd. When Cyrus grew to manhood in the land of Persis he revolted against his grandfather, whose army deserted to Cyrus.

Whatever the truth of this legend, about 550 BC, Cyrus inherited the kingdom of the Medes in Western Persia. He soon added to his territories by defeating Croesus, King of Lydia, and gaining the peaceful submission of Greek cities in what is now Turkey.

Cyrus' greatest conquest was that of the renowned city of Babylon, in October 539 BC. Most of the people of this great city were dissatisfied with the King, Nabondius, and welcomed Cyrus. He repaid their welcome by treating them well, and paying homage to their gods. He also released the Jews from their captivity in Babylon, and allowed them home. With Babylon, Cyrus acquired Mesopotamia, Syria and Palestine. His empire now stretched from the Mediterranean Sea to the Indus River on the borders of India, the largest empire ever known at that time.

Cyrus achieved this empire by a combination of skillful diplomacy, and military genius. His army of bowmen were a major factor in his success. His empire expanded under his dynasty, the Achaemnids, for two centuries, and this was largely a tribute to the wise way in which he administered his empire, showing tolerance towards the different practices of his subjects, and harbouring no grudges against those who had been his enemies. His reputation was passed on by the Persians to the Greeks, and greatly influenced the outlook of Alexander the Great, who was to build an empire in the same region.

Me tentarat avus vix natum exstinguere: contra
Ejus in exitium blandæ aluere feræ.

Sic erat in fatis; sibi quo servare putarat,
Hoc ipso vt Persis traderet imperium.

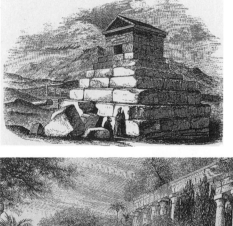

(Left) The triumphant Cyrus.
(Below) The tomb of Cyrus.
(Bottom) Babylon, captured by Cyrus, contained the Hanging Gardens, one of the Seven Wonders of the Ancient World.

Confucius

c.551–479 BC

For 2,000 years, the sayings and philosophy of Confucius shaped the society and culture of the Chinese people, the most populous race in the world. Although he did not try to found a religion, Confucius had a profound effect on the shape of Chinese religious practice which is still in evidence today.

The name Confucius is the Latin rendering of the Chinese K'ung Fu-tzu, which means Master Kung. Confucius grew up in the state of Lu (now Shantung), and after some years of poverty, earning a living as a labourer, became an accountant then a teacher. He took to wandering the countryside, discussing ethical problems with whoever he met. It is said that he met Lao-tzu, founder of another Chinese philosophy, Taoism. When civil war forced him to travel beyond his home province, his fame as a philosopher and teacher spread throughout China.

Confucius was always keen to find government office, and between 498 and 495 he served as prime minister to Duke Ting of Lu. His serious outlook did not please the frivolous duke, and Confucius had to resign, spending the next 13 years as a wandering teacher. The Duke's successor invited him back to revise some ancient scriptures, and Confucius died in Lu three years later.

In the course of his wanderings, Confucius had gathered a large following, and these disciples ensured his teachings lived on after him. They wrote his sayings in a number of books, most notably the *Analects*, and since Confucius himself wrote nothing, it is from these sources that we know his ideas.

Confucius taught that society depends on mutual respect, and the maintenance of established relationships on a basis of authority and obedience. This applied within the family, and between the ruler and the subject: indeed he held that all were part of one family. He urged submission to authority, but also that in return the ruler should follow this golden rule; "what you do not like when done to yourself do not do to others". He also counselled rulers to choose their advisors according to ability, even if their origin, like Confucius's, was humble, rather than because they were members of the "ruling class" by birth.

Since then, the Chinese have had a deep respect for the family. This respect has even extended as far as the worship of ancestors which is seen in Chinese society even today.

(Above) The meeting of the two great Chinese philosophers, Confucius and Lao-tzu, founder of Taoism.
"Master Kung". The influence of Confucianism was pre-eminent in China until the advent of communism in the present century. It particularly shaped Chinese attitudes towards authority and the family.

Buddha
c.560–486 BC

Buddhism was founded by Buddha in North India. It is a meditative religion, which teaches the pursuit of inner serenity, and has today some 70 million adherents.

The Buddha (which means "the enlightened one") was the son of the Rajah of the Sakya tribe in Kapilavastu, near Nepal in the foothills of the Himalayas. His name was Siddhartha Gautama. He has also been known as Sakya Muni, "sage of the Sakya". He was always of an other-wordly disposition, and his father arranged an early marriage for him to prevent him renouncing the world. Dissatisfied by the luxury of the court, Gautama made a number of attempts to see the outside world. During these he had four significant meetings; with an old man, a diseased man, a dead man, and a hermit.

After his son was born, he decided his duty had been done, and he left his sleeping wife and baby, his horses and chariots, shaved his head and set out to find the truth about the misery he had seen in his earlier encounters. Gautama tried a life of extreme self-denial, but did not find that this was the answer. After wrestling with temptation, he sat long in contemplation in the lotus position under a Bo (wild fig) tree at Buddh Gaya in Bihar. It was here that enlightenment came to him. It seemed to him that sorrow and suffering were the result of craving for life, and could only be defeated when such craving had been ended and a state of "nirvana" had been reached.

Buddha began to preach his new ideas, and soon attracted many disciples. He taught equality, brotherhood and the achievement of peace from suffering by self-sacrifice, contemplation, and the denial of passion. This would end the cycle of death and rebirth involved in the established Hindu idea that souls are reincarnated after death in another form.

His followers spent nine months of the year on the road, seeking new converts,

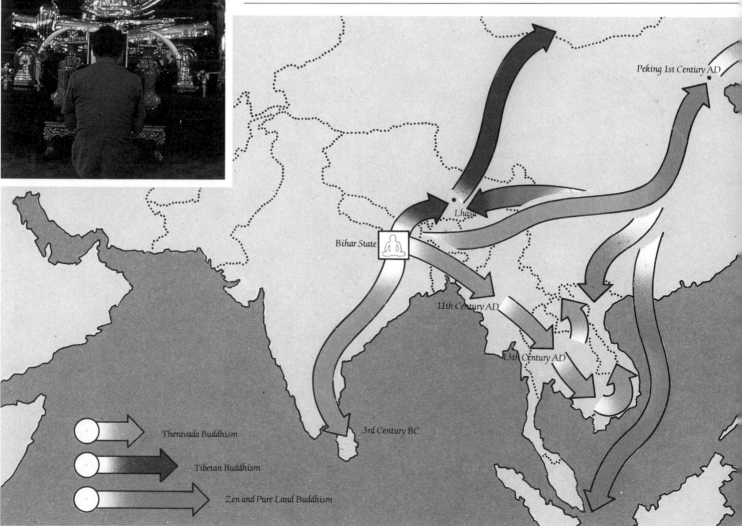

Bihar State

Lhasa

Peking 1st Century AD

11th Century AD

13th Century AD

3rd Century BC

Theravada Buddhism

Tibetan Buddhism

Zen and Pure Land Buddhism

possessing only their saffron robe and begging bowl, and three months in contemplation, first in caves, later in monasteries. They followed guidelines in meditation laid down by the Buddha, in what were known as the "three baskets" of sayings and discourses.

Buddha continued to journey around the countryside on foot. On one occasion he was attacked by a runaway elephant, which is said to have been calmed by the serenity of the master. Buddha died after 45 years of this work, aged about 80, and was buried at Kusinagara in Oudh, which is now a place of pilgrimage, though Buddha never claimed divinity for himself.

(Right) The temple of Athena, goddess of Athens, at Nike, c.427 BC.

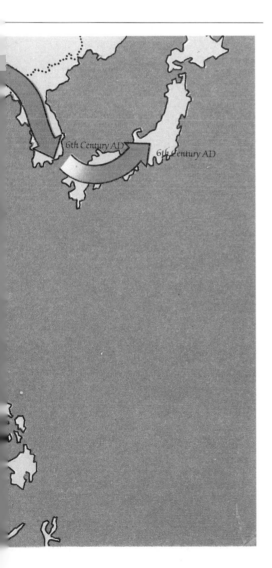

Socrates
c.469 399 BC

Socrates was the first and most original of the great Ancient Greek philosophers, who shaped the course of European ideas for 2,000 years.

Socrates was the son of a sculptor in the Greek city of Athens. He lived when Ancient Greek culture, the basis of European civilization, was at its height, centring upon a number of city states such as as Sparta, Thebes and Athens. For a time he was himself a sculptor. He later served with distinction as a soldier, and then spent the rest of his life in Athens in the markets and gymnasia. He would talk to anyone who would listen, and gathered around him a following of intelligent handsome young men, mostly sons of Athenian aristocrats. He himself was an ugly man, dressed in poor clothes: but he did not practise complete self-denial, for it is said that he could outdrink most of his companions!

Socrates's desire was that everyone should clearly know themselves, and clear their heads of muddled thoughts. He believed wickedness stemmed from ignorance, and that the achievement of knowledge would bring virtue. His method of achieving this was to address a series of progressively more probing questions to anyone he encountered, mercilessly exposing the deficiencies in his listener's ideas, and he hoped, to give them a clearer knowledge of themselves.

Socrates's scientific approach to philosophy and idealism was a great contribution to the future development of ideas, but in Ancient Athens his methods aroused the anger of those whose ignorance he exposed. His contempt for the traditional ways of life, and his questioning of conventions was too much for the Athenian nobles, who were suspicious of his following amongst their own sons. In 399 he was arrested and charged with blasphemy and corrupting the morals of the young. Socrates applied his methods to the judges of his trial, much to their distaste, and by a small majority was condemned to execution. He refused a chance to escape, and instead took poison, which was the customary alternative to execution.

His pupils Plato and Xenophon have related how Socrates spent his last hours, surrounded by his followers, discussing in matter-of-fact terms the slow effect the hemlock poison was having on him, and whether there was immortality. It was Plato to whom we owe most of our knowledge of Socrates's ideas. To Plato, a great philosopher in his own right, his teacher was the "wisest and most just and best of all men".

Alexander defeating King Darius of Persia at Issus in 333 BC. When he fled the field, Darius left his queen and family in Alexander's hands.

Alexander the Great
356–323 BC

Alexander the Great, King of Macedonia for only 13 years (336–323 BC), built one of the greatest empires the world has seen, and in the process spread Greek civilization far into Asia allowing a cross-fertilization of cultures which was to continue into the Roman era. Alexander was a brilliant military commander, but was not a destroyer, preferring to conserve and integrate the customs of the different areas he conquered. Alexander founded many cities; the most famous was Alexandria in Egypt. He is the central figure of many legends which have grown up during the centuries.

Alexander was the son of King Philip II of Macedon in Northern Greece. He was educated for a time by Aristotle, a pupil of Plato, and one of the first men to study nature systematically. During his campaign in Persia, he sent back many samples to his teacher. Alexander succeeded his father, who had been murdered, at the age of 20. He had already acquired a good reputation as a soldier, and he was able, with the army's help, to execute his father's assassins.

Philip had already established Macedonian control over the Greek cities, and when Thebes revolted, Alexander burnt it to the ground, with the exception of the temple and the house of the poet Pindar. Alexander was then free to turn to his great ambition, which was to

defeat the Persian empire that controlled the Greek cities in Asia Minor (Turkey) and for long had menaced Greece itself.

Alexander crossed the Hellespont strait into Asia in 334, and in a number of battles freed the Greek cities. As he marched to meet Darius, King of Persia, he came to the famous Gordian knot that a Phrygian king had tied round his chariot yoke so tightly no one could untie it. It was said that whoever did so would become ruler of the world. Characteristically, Alexander drew his sword and cut the knot.

Alexander used the same direct methods in fulfilling his design of conquering the Persian empire in which there were twenty times as many people

as in Greece. Alexander first conquered Syria and Egypt, and founded Alexandria. In brilliantly conducted battles at Gangamela, Granicus and Issus, he defeated Darius, who was finally murdered by his own dissatisfied troops.

Alexander was now able to enter the rich cities of Babylon and Susa, and the Persian capital Persepolis. He proclaimed himself lord of the world: he was in control of an area as large as the present-day United States. He pushed his conquests to the borders of India, marching in total 21,000 miles (33,800 km.). There he founded Bucephala, named after his horse Bucephalus, who died there. He defeated an Indian prince equipped with elephants, and would have marched into India, if his weary troops, after eight years campaigning, had not refused to go any farther.

As the Greek and Persian worlds were now united under Alexander's rule his next intention was to fuse the two cultures. His first step was a mass marriage of himself and his men with Persian women. He adopted Persian dress, and tried to have his men treat him like a god, as was the custom in the East, but this met with laughter from the practical-minded Greeks.

Many legends grew up around Alexander, during and after his lifetime. The truth is that he was a man of great qualities, and great weaknesses. A brilliant commander and statesman, tolerant of other civilizations, he was also vain and suspicious, and prone to violent drunken fits. During one of these he killed his best friend Clitus, and on other

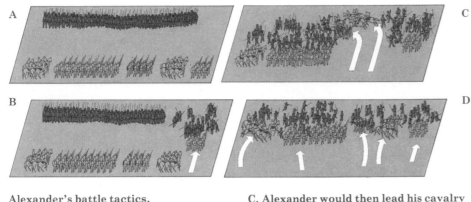

Alexander's battle tactics.

A. The phalanx – a large body of foot soldiers – was placed in the centre.

B. Alexander began battle by attacking on the extreme right.

C. Alexander would then lead his cavalry and household troops into the gap.

D. His cavalry could then fall on the exposed flank while the phalanx engaged the main force.

The empire of Alexander the Great.

occasions had many of his closest associates executed. It was after a bout of drinking that he contracted a fever and died at the age of 33, with the world at his feet.

His empire was split up between his generals on his death, but the Greek-speaking world, stretching from Gibraltar to India persisted, which helped both the expansion of the later Roman Empire, and the spread of Christianity.

Hannibal
247–183 BC

Hannibal of Carthage was one of the greatest generals of the Ancient world. His renowned crossing of the Alps with elephants resulted in the Romans' heaviest defeat.

Carthage was a city in North Africa and a rival of Rome. At the age of nine, Hannibal, the son of a general, was made to swear perpetual enmity to Rome.

When he was 26, Hannibal became Carthaginian commander in Spain. In 218 BC, Hannibal left Cartagena in Spain with 50,000 infantry, 9,000 cavalry and 37 elephants, crossed the Rhône River and headed into the Alps mountains.

It was already autumn when Hannibal began to cross the Alps. His men, from Africa and Spain, were little used to cold and snow. The paths were narrow and icy. They were attacked by the natives who rolled rocks down on them. Many were lost by falling, and many more from cold and hunger. Hannibal shared his men's privations, and his spirit and leadership kept them going. After 15 days they descended into Italy.

This was one of the great feats of military history, achieved at the cost of between five to ten thousand men and most of the elephants. Hannibal had caught the Romans off guard, and he proceeded to destroy their armies at Trebia, Ticino and Lake Trasimene.

For a time the Romans avoided further battle, but in 216 BC finally confronted him at Cannae, and Hannibal scored his greatest victory. By his use of cavalry he surrounded the Romans, who far outnumbered him, and slew about 56,000 out of 80,000, the worst defeat in Roman history. Many of the highest Roman citi-

Hannibal crossing the Rhône on rafts.

zens were killed, and it is said Hannibal sent a bushel of their gold rings home.

Hannibal campaigned in Italy for 15 years, but was unable to take the fortified city of Rome. In 203 BC he had to return to face a Roman attack on Carthage. He was decisively defeated at Zama. Rome now dominated the Mediterranean. Hannibal entered the Carthaginian government, but the Romans hated him and he was forced to flee, first to Syria, then Bithynia (North West Turkey). The Romans continued to hunt him down, and to avoid capture, Hannibal took poison.

(Left) The death of Caesar.
(Above) The splendours of Ancient Rome now form picturesque ruins, which have inspired many subsequent generations.

Julius Caesar

c.100–44 BC

Gaius Julius Caesar was a Roman general, author and statesman. His victories extended Roman rule to the river Rhine. He took absolute control in Rome in 45 BC, ending the ineffective rule of the Senate and establishing one-man absolute rule, which ushered in Rome's golden age. He was murdered the following year.

Caesar was born of a Roman patrician family, which was neither rich nor powerful. Caesar hid his serious self under a mask of light-hearted gaiety, and was a favourite of the common people. In 66 BC, as overseer of the public games, he presented magnificent spectacles in the Great Circus in Rome, at considerable personal expense. Caesar saw the ineffectiveness of the government of Rome by the nobles in the Senate, and believed a strong central power was needed to revive Roman greatness. He formed an alliance, the Triumvirate, with the two most powerful men in Rome, Crassus and Pompey. As a result, he was elected Consul (the chief Roman magistrate) in 59 BC.

Traditionally, Consuls served in the provinces after their year in office. Caesar became Proconsul in Cisalpine Gaul (North Italy). There he built up a highly trained, well-disciplined army, which became devoted to Caesar. He conquered Transalpine Gaul (France). He also raided Britain, though he did not attempt to conquer it. He shared the hardships of campaigning with his men, and put down a mutiny by shaming his troops with the declaration that he and his faithful Tenth Legion would fight on alone if necessary. His account of the campaign, written in his litter on the march is a classic.

The Triumvirate broke up with the death of Crassus, and Pompey, distrustful of Caesar's popularity, moved to the side of the Senate. Caesar was told to disband his army. Fearing he would then be attacked, Caesar refused to do so, and crossed the Rubicon river dividing his province from Italy proper. This amounted to a declaration of war. The ensuing civil war lasted five years, with fighting in Spain, Africa and Asia Minor. Pompey was killed in Egypt, where Caesar met Queen Cleopatra, whom he took back to Rome as his mistress. After victories in Asia, Caesar sent back his famous message, "I came, I saw, I conquered".

Caesar returned to Rome, now in absolute control. He widened representation in the Senate, and extended citizenship to conquered peoples. He reformed the calendar; the month July is named after him. He had only a year's rule as dictator. Caesar refused a crown, but supporters of the old republic, together with some of his followers scared by his great power, conspired to kill him.

The Senate met on March 15, the Ides of March in the Roman calendar, and Caesar was warned by a soothsayer not to attend. He went regardless, and was stabbed to death by 60 conspirators. On seeing his friend Brutus amongst them, he said. "Et tu, Brute" (you too, Brutus) and gave up the struggle, dying under Pompey's statue.

Caesar's death sealed his victory, for after five more years of war, Octavius Caesar, his adopted son, secured power and took the name Augustus. A long and fruitful period of personal rule began.

Jesus Christ

c.4 BC–c.AD 30

Jesus Christ, who spent all his life in Palestine, was the founder of the Christian religion, which now has 900 million adherents in every continent of the world. Christians claim that Jesus was not only the "Messiah", the saviour spoken of in the Old Testament of the Bible, but was God in human form.

Jesus's story is told in the four Gospels of the New Testament. He was born in a stable in Bethlehem, where his mother Mary and her husband, Joseph, who was a descendant of King David, had come for the census. Jesus was raised as a Jewish boy in the town of Nazareth, and was taught Joseph's trade, that of carpenter. Palestine at that time was part of the Roman Empire, ruled by Augustus Caesar, Julius's successor.

At the age of about 30, Jesus began to preach, and gathered about him twelve close disciples, simple fishermen and others of humble origin. Jesus's message was simple, and very attractive to the poor and the oppressed. He preached that God is Love, and that anyone could get to Heaven, so long as they followed simple precepts; to love their enemies and to forgive others as they wished to be forgiven themselves. He angered the established religious leaders by claiming to be the Messiah, the son of God, and declaring that sincerity, not outward adherence to the forms of the Jewish religion was important. He angered the rich by declaring that they should give

(Above left) Jesus and his mother, the Virgin Mary.
(Above) Da Vinci's sketch, *The Saviour*.
(Right) The Crucifixion.

their wealth up and follow him. The poor were attracted by the healing of the sick and the message of equality in the eyes of God for those who repented.

After entering Jerusalem to the acclaim of the crowd, Jesus was betrayed to the priests in the garden of Gethsemane by Judas Iscariot, one of the twelve. They took him to the Roman governor, Pontius Pilate, who was afraid of Jesus's popularity and of the cries of the crowd egged on by the priests. Jesus was executed by crucifixion on a charge of blasphemy.

Christians claim that three days later, on Easter Day, his tomb was found empty, and Jesus appeared alive to his disciples in a locked room. One, known as "doubting Thomas", had to touch Jesus's wounds made by the nails of the cross before he believed. Jesus had conquered death, and had reconciled God and man separated by man's wrongdoing. This was the message Christians carried as their faith spread through the Empire. They were persecuted at first but under Emperor Constantine Christianity became the official religion of the Roman Empire from Britain to Egypt.

Boadicea
d.AD 61

Boadicea was Britain's first national hero. She was Queen of a tribe of Ancient Britons, the Iceni, and led a revolt against their Roman conquerors in AD 61. After sacking Colchester, London and St Albans, she was defeated, and died after the battle.

The Romans invaded Britain in AD 43. They soon reduced southern England to a Roman province, as they had done earlier in Gaul (France) and Hispania (Spain). One Roman method of maintaining control over their subject peoples was to grant land to retiring soldiers of their army, instead of pay. They followed this policy in Britannia (Britain) too, and it was this that was at the root of the Iceni revolt. The Iceni were a populous tribe inhabiting present day Norfolk, Suffolk, Huntingdonshire and Cambridgeshire. While the governor, Suetonius Paulus was campaigning in the north, these ex-soldiers stole farms from the Iceni, including lands belonging to the late King, Prasutagus. The royal house was invaded and pillaged. Queen Boadicea was whipped and her daughters attacked.

Boadicea was not the woman to take such treatment, and she took to her chariot, with her back still sore from the scourging. The East Anglias rose behind her. She led a great army of men and women towards the centre of Roman settlement in south-east England. Camulodunum (Colchester), Londinium (London) and Verulamium (St Albans) were burnt to the ground. At Verulamium, the capital, 70,000 Romans and British collaborators were killed.

Suetonius returned and in a long, savage battle, the trained soldiers won the day, and thousands of Britons died.

Boadicea took her life by poison rather than once more fall into the hands of the Romans. The Iceni revolt was the most serious the Romans had to face in Britain. After Boadicea was defeated, the Romans had little further trouble in bringing Britain, as far north as the border with Scotland, under their control. On the border they built Hadrian's Wall to keep the warlike Scots out. Britain gained much from Roman civilization, but Boadicea is still remembered as a symbol of resistance to invasion. She is commemorated in a statue by Westminster Bridge in London, facing the Houses of Parliament, at the reins of her famous chariot.

Boadicea's statue, Westminster, London. She is one of Britain's earliest heroes.

Attila the Hun
c.406–53

Attila was the most famous leader of the Huns, one of the tribes of barbarians which despoiled the Roman Empire. Attila acquired a reputation for destruction second to none, and the nickname "scourge of God".

The great Roman Empire was destroyed by the attacks of tribes of warlike barbarians who originated in Mongolia and central Asia. The Huns had begun to enter Europe in the 4th century AD, and were brave, merciless warriors, mounted on rugged little ponies. Attila and his brother Bleda inherited an empire stretching from the Baltic Sea and the Alps to the Caspian Sea, with control

One of many fierce and bloody battles
between Attila's Huns and the Romans.
Successive waves of barbarians swept
into the Roman Empire.
All except the restless Huns remained to
settle alongside the inhabitants.

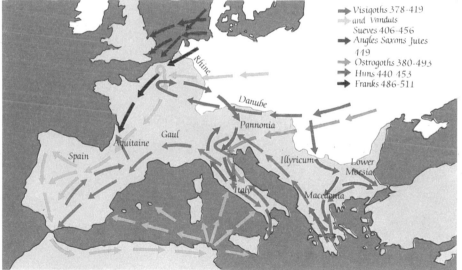

Visigoths 378-419
and Vandals
Sueves 406-456
Angles Saxons Jutes
449
Ostrogoths 380-493
Huns 440 453
Franks 486-511

over a number of territories of the
Eastern Roman Empire, which paid
them tribute to keep the peace.

In 445, Attila murdered his brother
and ruled alone. In 451 he invaded Gaul
(France), a Roman province inhabited by
Visigoths, earlier invaders who had
settled there and adopted Roman ways.
Attila had received a plea from Honoria,
the sister of Emperor Valentinian III, to
rescue her from a marriage arranged for
her against her will. Attila claimed her
for himself, and invaded Gaul on her
behalf, in hopes of winning half the
Western Roman Empire as dowry.

Attila's hordes swept through Gaul,
looting and plundering. He was unable
to capture Aureliarum (Orléans), and
retired after being defeated, for the only
time in his life, at the battle of Maurica.
He had the consolation that Theodoric,
the Visigoth king was killed.

The next campaigning season, in 452,
Attila invaded Italy and sacked a host of
cities in the North. It was only the
famine and plague that were also ravag-
ing north Italy at the time, that stopped
him carrying his campaign to Rome
itself.

Attila planned to renew his campaign
of terror the following year, but he died
in his sleep on the night following his
marriage, a strangely peaceful ending
for a savage warrior. He was buried with
his treasures, and the gravediggers were
then murdered so that his grave would
never be discovered.

Attila was an autocratic, blustering
man, uninterested in any of the trap-
pings of civilization, even to the extent
that he ate off wooden plates while his
officers ate off plundered silver. Attila's
name is still used to call up images of
unrivalled savagery fifteen centuries
later, despite the shortness of his active
career.

Gregory the Great

c.540–604

Pope Gregory the Great (Gregory I) was the last of the great Fathers of the Roman Catholic Church. He is best remembered as the initiator of the conversion of England to Christianity.

By Gregory's time the Roman Empire in Western Europe had finally succumbed to the barbarian invasions. The Eastern Empire survived, centring on Constantinople (now Istanbul), and it controlled parts of south Italy, but was too far away to protect Rome effectively.

Gregory was the grandson of a previous pope, Felix III, and a man of noble family and wealth. He was however, modest and retiring, and having founded and endowed a monastery in Rome, joined it himself. He remained a monk for the rest of his life.

In 590 Gregory was made pope, despite his vigorous objections that he was unworthy of the office. He had three main aims as pope; to relieve the sufferings of the people, particularly refugees fleeing from the invading Lombards, to convert the heathens to Roman Christianity, and to establish the authority of the papacy in the west. In all of these he was successful. He gained a reputation as a "people's pope", using Church funds to help the poor, and it is said he was canonised (made a saint) by popular acclaim.

Gregory made papal administration more efficient in order to distribute help to the poor. One result of doing so was to enhance the power of the office of pope, particularly over central Italy, which became known as the Papal States. By taking a leading role in converting the barbarians, he further extended papal authority, and by the end of his reign the papacy was exercising much of the power in the west that had fallen from the hands of the weak Eastern Emperors.

It is said that Gregory's interest in Britain was first aroused by seeing some handsome British slave boys in a Roman market. On asking who they were, he was told Angles (an English tribe): he answered "not Angles, but Angels". In 596 he made the greatest act of his papacy by sending St Augustine to be the first Archbishop of Canterbury, and convert the English. In this Augustine was so successful, that it was to be English missionaries, led by St Boniface, who undertook the conversion of the populous German tribes, less than a hundred years later.

Gregory popularized the church service, instituting the lovely Gregorian chants. This all helped to increase the influence of the papacy, and its claim to the leadership of the whole Christian Church. Gregory remained modest, and forbade veneration of his tomb on pain of excommunication. Such was the popularity of the "people's pope" that this was one of the few of his orders to be disobeyed.

Pope Gregory lying on his couch, teaching Roman boys the chant which still bears his name. He established a school of singing, supported by the produce of two farms. His couch, and the scourge used to punish the boys, were preserved after his death.

Legend

- Mohammed's conquests to 632
- Expansion of Islam to 661
- Expansion of Islam to 750
- Expansion of Islam to 945

Mohammed
c.570–632

Mohammed was the prophet of the religion of Islam, which today has some 500 million adherents. He also united the Arab tribes into a great state, which was eventually to stretch from Spain to India.

Mohammed was a wealthy merchant in the city of Mecca in Arabia on the Red Sea coast. He was always of reflective mind, and in about 610, he received a vision of the angel Gabriel, who said to him, "You are the Messenger of God". He had further revelations, which came in the form of messages rather than pictorial visions, and after his death these came to be set down in the holy book of Islam, the *Qu'ran (Koran)*. With the help of a Christian cousin of his wife Khadijah, he interpreted these as similar to messages sent by God through prophets to Jews and Christians, and that he was now commanded to communicate the will of God to the Arabs.

In 613 he began to preach in Mecca, soon gathering a following of young men. In contrast to the worship of many gods in Mecca he taught "Islam" (submission to one God) and his followers became known as "Muslims" (those who submit). He declared that riches came from God, and that those who had them should show their gratitude by generosity. This aroused opposition amongst the merchants, and in 622 he was forced to make the "Hegira", or emigration, just escaping a plot to kill him, and finally settling in Medina.

Mohammed's followers gathered around him in Medina, and organised raids on Meccan trading caravans. By a series of marriages (nine in all), Mohammed gained many allies amongst the various clans. An attack by Mecca was beaten off in 627, due to Mohammed's defensive preparations, and every success brought more adherents to his cause and his faith.

In 628 he went on pilgrimage to Mecca, and hostilities were ended by treaty; when this treaty was broken by the Meccans in 630, Mohammed took the city by force. He destroyed the Meccan idols, and many more became Muslims. After defeating hostile nomads at the battle of Hunayn in 631, Mohammed was now master of Arabia.

By his simple message that God rewards the faithful and condemns the faithless, Mohammed had succeeded in uniting the warring Arab tribes. He ended the practice of the blood feud, which had brought much warfare by involving a whole tribe in a murder committed by one of its members. He also succeeded in ending infanticide (murder of babies).

In order to prevent Muslim fighting Muslim, Mohammed directed the great energies and zeal of the Arabs outwards, leading an attack on the Syrian frontier of the Eastern Roman Empire in 632. In that year, Mohammed died while on pilgrimage to Mecca; he left the Arab Muslim world poised for an expansion that would take Islam to the borders of France, deep into Africa and to India and beyond in Asia.

Charlemagne

742–814

Charlemagne (from the Latin Carolus Magnus, Charles the Great) was king of the Franks from 768, and Holy Roman Emperor from 800. He restored the Roman Empire in the West, and encouraged a revival of learning and art, known as the Carolingian Renaissance.

Charlemagne was King of the Franks, a former barbarian tribe that had settled in Gaul (France) during the Roman Empire and had adopted the Christian religion. He succeeded his father, the ambitious Pepin the Short, who had made himself king in place of the weak rulers his family had long served. Frankish custom was that inheritances were divided equally amongst all sons: this happened with Pepin's heirs, and caused much trouble, until Charlemagne's brother Carloman died in 771. Carloman's sons fell into Charlemagne's hands and disappeared.

Charlemagne had campaigned at his father's side and shared his father's readiness to fight to extend his power. He first conquered the Lombards of north Italy, whose ruler had supported Carloman.

Charlemagne fought the Saxons, Bavarians and Alemanii in Germany, and the Avars in Hungary, and brought all the Germanic tribes in western Europe under his sway. He converted them to Roman Catholic Christianity, sometimes by peaceful, sometimes by violent means. The empire which he created seemed to contemporaries to be a revival of the old Roman Empire, though now based on Christianity, and on Frankish customs. In 800 he was crowned Holy Roman Emperor in Rome by the Pope. Charlemagne however kept his capital in the heart of Frankish territory at Aachen, in modern Belgium.

Charlemagne also campaigned in Spain against the Muslim Moors. On the first occasion, Arab envoys from Spain asked his help against their overlord the Emir of Cordoba, but he was defeated at Zaragosa. During the retreat, one of his officers, Roland, was killed after a heroic

The medieval shrine of Charlemagne at Aix-la-Chapelle.

The empire of Charlemagne. It was split up in his grandsons' time.

stand that became the subject of many songs and stories in the Middle Ages. Later, Charlemagne returned to Spain, and in 801, captured Barcelona from the Moors.

Charlemagne's reign saw the beginning of the end of the Dark Ages of European civilization. Although he could not write, and read little, Charlemagne encouraged the spread of learning and the arts, which was a crucial contribution to the development of a specifically European culture.

Charlemagne established for the first time a sense of unity within Christian Europe, missing since Roman times, and this endured, as did Charlemagne's reputation as the ideal Christian ruler. However, such an extensive empire at a time of poor communications needed an exceptional to man to hold it together, and within a generation it split apart.

Alfred burning the cakes in the herdswoman's hut.

Alfred the Great
849–99

Alfred, King of Wessex, was the only English king ever to be called "the Great". He defeated and ejected the Danish invaders from the south-east of England. He was a wise lawgiver, and a patron of culture; he brought about a revival of English learning and set an example with his own writings.

England in Alfred's time was perpetually menaced by invasion by the Vikings from Scandinavia; most of them were Danes, who aimed to conquer the country, rather than simply raid. Almost all of the eastern part of England was occupied by them. Half of Alfred's kingdom of Wessex (land of the West Saxons) was in their hands. Alfred set himself the task of driving them out. He suffered many setbacks; once having to hide after a surprise attack in the Somerset marshes. Legend has it that he was so preoccupied with his problems that while sheltering in a peasant woman's hut he allowed some cakes he was minding to burn.

Alfred finally defeated the Danes at Ethandune in 878, and even succeeded in converting their leader, Guthrun, to Christianity. He established his capital at Winchester, and went on to expel the Danes from London in 885–86. This feat, which left only parts of East Anglia and the north-east in Danish hands, won the acclaim of other English rulers, and he was recognized as overlord of all England.

Alfred was far more than just a successful soldier. In spite of the need to be on permanent guard against renewed attacks, and to build English defences in the form of forts and ships, Alfred found time to sponsor and encourage a remarkable flowering of English culture. He himself learnt to read and write, and translated works of the Church philosophers, Augustine of Hippo and Boethius into English. This was quite remarkable for a warrior king. He instructed all young nobles to learn to read, for he believed the Viking raids were punishment for wickedness and ignorance.

Alfred took his kingship seriously, and revised English laws, while not attempting to alter established customs. He attracted great devotion and loyalty. Throughout the Middle Ages he was regarded as the king who defeated an invader who had superior forces, a wise lawgiver, and the epitome of the ideal king. It is doubtful if there has been an abler king of England.

King Canute

994–1035

Canute, or Cnut, was King of England from 1016. He was a Dane, and incorporated England into an empire that included Denmark and Norway. He was a wise ruler, most famous for his demonstration of the limits of kingly power.

Canute began his career in England as a typical Viking. For two centuries, these raiding warriors had sought to conquer England. Canute came over in 1013 with his father, King Sweyn Forkbeard, and continued the struggle on Sweyn's death in 1014. He was quite ruthless: when he was forced to retreat, he left his hostages at Sandwich, horribly mutilated. On his return, when Earl Uhtred submitted to him, Canute had him murdered in his own home.

The English king, Ethelread the Unraed (ill-advised; often mistranslated as "Unready") died in 1016, and the Witan (the council of nobles) elected Canute king. This proved a far-sighted choice. At first the kingdom was divided with Ethelread's son, Edmund Ironside, but his death in November 1016 left Canute undisputed king. Canute at first killed or outlawed the English nobles, and put Danes into their estates.

However, the civilization, prosperity and religion of England soon had a remarkable effect. Canute became a devout Christian, and made a pilgrimage to Rome, where he earned the respect of the Pope and Emperor (and also concessions for English traders). He dismissed most of the Danish fleet, and brought peace and prosperity to England, such as it had not known since the Viking raids started.

Canute had a high idea of his duties as a ruler, but was well aware of his limitations. Flattering courtiers suggested he was so great that the waves would obey his commands. Canute had his throne set on the beach, and when the tide approached, ordered the sea to fall back. When the water ran over his feet, he said to the flatterers, "Let all men know how empty and worthless is the power of kings; for there is none worthy of the name but Him whom heaven, earth and sea obey."

Canute inherited the kingdom of Denmark, and conquered Norway. England became part of the Scandinavian world, and closely involved in trade in the Baltic. Canute's achievement rested on the strength of his character, and under his sons Harold and Hardicanute, it fell apart. England returned to Saxon rule under Ethelread's son Edward the Confessor.

(Left) The hardy Vikings crossed the oceans in open ships like this, sailing as far as America. (Below right) Canute reproves his flattering courtiers.

Chao K'ang-yin
d.976

Chao K'ang-yin, also known as T'ai Tsu (Great Founder or Father), was Emperor of China 960–976. He united the Ten Kingdoms of China and founded the S'ung dynasty, which lasted to 1280, a time when Chinese culture flourished.

Since the demise of the T'ang dynasty 100 years before, China had broken up into the Ten Kingdoms, and authority rested with many warlords. The actual Emperor had little power over these independent lords, who had strong armies. This only changed when one actually became Emperor himself. Chao was commander of the capital, Chang-an, and used his military power to overthrow the Emperor.

Chao did not destroy the other powerful generals, but granted them high-sounding titles and offices with large pensions. Chao's success brought a more peaceful climate to China, and Chinese culture flowered.

Chao's descendants were known as the S'ung dynasty, and their era is renowned as a high point in the long history of Chinese civilization. Under the S'ung, gunpowder was invented and used in firecrackers. Printing with carved blocks was developed. Literature, both prose and poetry, thrived. It was a specially creative period in porcelain pottery, an art in which the Chinese have excelled. Confucianism was refined into a nationwide philosophy. A distinctly Chinese culture grew up.

There was a price to pay for this. To the north, China was threatened by powerful neighbours. These were kept relatively peaceful by tribute of money, but it was an insecure peace. The reforms in the long term weakened the military prowess of the Chinese, and their ability to keep these enemies at bay. In the lifetime of Chao, his own abilities as a general more than compensated.

Chao lived according to the doctrines of Confucius, ruling humanely and listening to the advice of his ministers. His reputation eased his declared aim of reunifying the country, for many were happy to live under his rule. Together with his political skill, the strength of his hand-picked soldiers, and the fact that he treated defeated rivals generously, this assured him of success. The last of the Ten Kingdoms surrendered without a fight in 978. By that time, Chao had died. It was rumoured that he had been assassinated, but his sudden death was probably the result of heavy drinking.

Art of the Sung Dynasty; birds and flowers on cut silk.

William the Conqueror
1027–1087

William the Conqueror was King of England from 1066 to 1087. He introduced Norman French culture and society to England. He was victor of the battle of Hastings, 1066, which gave him the English crown. He was responsible for the compilation of the Domesday Book in 1086, a record of the realm of England and her people.

William was the illegitimate son of Robert, Duke of Normandy, and succeeded to the dukedom at the age of eight, when his father died while returning from a pilgrimage to Jerusalem. The Normans were a tough warlike people, related to the Vikings, who had settled in the North of France. There was much disorder in Normandy during William's youth, and he had great difficulty in holding on to his dukedom. Three of his guardians died violent deaths, and his tutor was murdered. William learnt from these experiences to be hard and ruthless.

By 1060, William had mastered his unruly barons, and began to turn his attention to the expansion of his territories, both within France, and across the English Channel. William was related to the King of England, the saintly Edward the Confessor, who was childless, and gained a promise from Edward that he would succeed him. Edward had no right to make that promise, for the Anglo-Saxons of England elected their kings. The tradition was that the great nobles would meet in a council called the Witan and select one of their number, usually, but not always, a relative of the king. The most powerful of the nobles was Earl Godwin of Wessex. Godwin's son Harold fought with William in Brittany, and during this campaign William claimed that Harold promised on a box of holy relics that he would support an attempt by William to be king. Harold claimed the promise was got from him by trickery.

When Edward died, Harold was elected king. William decided to try to conquer England by force. Harold's half-brother Tostig, in league with the King of Norway attempted an invasion at the same time, though the two attacks were probably not coordinated. William hoped to land in the south of England while Harold was occupied fighting Tostig in the north, but encountered bad weather on the Channel, and lost a number of ships. Just when it seemed best to give up, a comet was sighted (later called Halley's Comet), and this was taken as a good omen. The winds changed, and the Normans were able to land near Hastings on the English south coast.

Harold hastened south to meet

The world of William the Conqueror is illustrated in two unique records. The Bayeux tapestry (above) depicts the battle of Hastings. The Normans are shown here landing in England. The Domesday Book (below) is a remarkably detailed survey of English life 1,000 years ago.

William, having defeated Tostig at Stamford Bridge in Yorkshire. A decisive battle took place near Hastings, at a place now called Battle. William won by his persistence, for the Anglo-Saxon shield wall proved very successful against his attacks. It was only when the discipline of his enemy broke, and they charged forward in the belief they had won, that William's archers were able to win the day. The battle was vividly recorded by Norman ladies in the famous Bayeux tapestry. Harold was hit in the eye with an arrow, and killed. William marched to London, and on Christmas Day 1066 was crowned. During the ceremony, William's guards mistook shouts of acclaim for an attack and rushed in, killing many and abruptly terminating the service.

It was to take William another five years to gain full control of his new realm, laying great areas in the north waste in the process, and developing a dislike for his new kingdom and its people. After the defeat of the last Anglo-Saxon stronghold, that of Hereward the Wake on the Isle of Ely, the old English aristocracy had been almost completely wiped out. William made his followers the new lords over the English. He instituted the Norman feudal system of rigidly defined relationships between ruler and ruled, to enable his men to maintain their control and supply him with soldiers from among

their peasants when he needed them. William built castles to keep the land subdued; the greatest was the White Tower, which still stands as the keep of the Tower of London.

William was to spend much of the rest of his reign in Normany, defending his lands against other nobles, and his rebellious son, Robert Curthose. He returned to England only when it was in danger. On one of these occasions, an expected invasion from Denmark did not happen, and instead William ordered the compilation of the Domesday Book, the first census of England. Monks and royal officials went around the countryside and noted exactly who owned what piece of land, the size of villages, and the mode of life of the inhabitants, so that William would know exactly what he owned. Under the feudal system, all the realm ultimately belonged to the king, though nobles were granted lordships in return for rendering him services, in the same way that the peasants (serfs) received the use of land in return for serving their master.

William was a masterful, ruthless man, who was feared and respected. Although he was cruel and avaricious, he had a strict concern for law and order, probably as a result of his perilous boyhood, and this made his government firm but fair. He was a hunter and soldier and continued in those pursuits till the end of his life, despite becoming quite fat. His introduction of a French-speaking aristocracy and the feudal system was a turning point in English history. William died in battle in Normandy in 1087, and his realm was split between his sons William Rufus (England) and Robert (Normandy), but the relationship of England with affairs in France remained close, with lasting effects on English culture, particularly language.

King John
c.1167–1216

John was the youngest of the three sons of Henry II, the first Plantagenet King (1154–89), who ruled an extensive empire including Aquitaine and Normandy as well as England. His sons were so unruly that they were known as the "devil's brood".

While John's brother, King Richard the Lionheart (1189–99) was away on crusade, John tried to seize control of England, and plotted to keep Richard from returning. He failed, and had his lands taken from him, gaining him the name "Lackland".

The King later forgave him, and John succeeded him as King in 1199. John secured his claim to the throne by the murder of his brother Geoffrey's son Arthur, a twelve year old boy and claimant to the throne, in 1203.

John was an able administrator, but a poor soldier, and lost his French inheritance to King Philip Augustus of France in 1204–05. John's disastrous reign then saw a long dispute with Pope Innocent III, over the choice of the Archbishop of Canterbury. John was excommunicated, and England put under a Papal Ban; no

John was King of England, 1199–1216. During his rule the Magna Carta was signed in 1215.

church services, baptisms, weddings or burials could be held. John finally had to give way, and made a humiliating surrender.

The expense of all John's failures drove him to assert royal rights that his predecessors had ignored. John was the first king for many years to spend most of his time in England. He travelled around the country raising money, and was not particular about the method he used. He was a selfish, vain man, given to violent fits of temper, in which it is said he foamed at the mouth and bit branches. He caused much comment by

King John signs Magna Carta, Runnymede, 1215.

his habit of taking regular baths, very unusual for the time.

In order to curb his excesses, the barons, supported by the clergy and other citizens, forced John to sign Magna Carta (the Great Charter), at Runnymede on the Thames in 1215. This made clear the king was subject to the law, and gave rights to subjects against arbitrary imprisonment and financial extortion. It has influenced democratic systems in Britain and other English-speaking countries. An original copy is kept permanently in the United States.

John quickly ignored the promises he had made, and in desperation the barons called on Louis, son of Philip Augustus, to be king. John fought on, and during the campaign was caught in the marshy area in Norfolk, called the Wash, and lost the crown jewels. Soon afterwards, he died, alone and almost friendless, and probably poisoned.

Genghis Khan
c.1167–1227

Genghis Khan was chief of the Mongol tribes of North-East Asia from 1180. A warrior and ruler of genius, he conquered an empire which stretched 4,000 miles (6,450 km), from Turkey to China. With a reputation for savagery rarely equalled, he was the terror of the Arab and Christian worlds.

The Mongol peoples inhabited an area to the north of the Great Wall of China, which was built to keep them out. The Mongols were nomads, moving to wherever there was pasture for their hardy ponies. They were warlike, but used up a lot of their energies fighting amongst themselves. Genghis' great achievement was to weld them into a nation and bring them under a rigid military discipline.

Genghis Khan's original name was Temujin, after an enemy his father had just killed when his son was born. His father, a clan leader, was poisoned when Temujin was nine, and he and his mother lived in poverty. Once he was captured by the new ruling family, and made to wear a wooden yoke. He escaped by knocking down his guard with the yoke, while the others were feasting. When he grew older, he won control of his tribe, and destroyed those who had humiliated him.

Temujin used his military genius to destroy rival tribes; he would slaughter all the nobles, and take the common people into his own forces. This way all Mongols were united behind his family. A special vengeance was reserved for the Tartars, who had murdered his father: all those who were taller than a cart axle were killed. This left only the children alive, and they were absorbed into Temujin's own tribe.

By 1206 his dominance was complete, and at a great assembly of tribes he was declared "Genghis Khan" (Universal King). The Mongols flooded into China, taking Peking in 1215. They then attacked the Muslim kingdom of Khwarezm in Afghanistan, and began to acquire their reputation for savagery. Defeated peoples would be massacred, or

Ancient manuscript showing Mongol troops crossing a frozen river.

forced to march in front of the Mongols into battle against their own kin. The Mongols' reputation paralysed resistance, but even a quick surrender did not always prevent the entire populations of cities being laid out in the sand and beheaded. Genghis originally saw China as new grazing land for his ponies. As he gained knowledge of other ways of life, his ideas became more sophisticated. He saw that a settled peasantry like that in China could provide a steady supply of money, in taxes, of more lasting value than mere plunder. Similarly, he adapted his mode of fighting to suit conditions, developing weapons to capture towns. It was this

adaptibility that was the key to his success.

Genghis died when his army was on the brink of further expansion. Under his son Ogodai, and grandson Kublai, the Mongols conquered all of China and Persia, and most of Russia, creating a tightly knit empire. Neighbouring peoples were in perpetual terror of their further advance, and the name of Genghis Khan has become a byword for destruction and savagery.

Wat Tyler
d.1381

Wat Tyler was the leader of the first great popular rebellion in England in 1381. It was called the Peasants Revolt.

In 1349 the Black Death ravaged the English countryside. A third of the population was carried off by this terrible plague. This produced a great shortage of labour, and the English peasants found themselves much in demand, and the old feudal system by which peasants were virtually the property of one lord broke down. To the lords, it seemed like the traditional order in the country was under threat, and harsh measures were passed by them in Parliament to reassert their control.

The situation was aggravated by the fact that the government needed money to pay for a war in France, and imposed a tax of one shilling per head on each person, regardless of income. In many areas the tax collectors were chased out of town. Radical preachers, known as hedge-priests, who had become a common sight in 14th century England, circulated between the villages, preaching equality for peasants, and stirring them to revolt.

In Kent the rebels gathered round Wat

The Burning of St. John's Monastry near Smithfield, by Wat Tyler's Mob.

Tyler, whose origins are obscure, though it is reputed that he was a highwayman. He led them to free John Ball, a prominent hedge-priest, from Maidstone prison, and to capture Canterbury on June 10 1381. They then marched to London, where sympathetic townsmen let them into the City. They claimed to wish to rid the King of bad advisors, such as his uncle, John of Gaunt. They ransacked Gaunt's house, the Savoy

Palace; nothing was stolen, and a man who tried to do so was beaten.

Essex rebels had meanwhile arrived at Mile End outside the city. The King, Richard II, a boy of 14, bravely rode out to meet them, and agreed to liberate the peasants. Tyler's men took the Tower of London, and killed the Chancellor, Sudbury, the Treasurer, Hales, and other royal officials.

On June 15 the Kentish rebels, still well organized despite the disorders in the City, met the King at Smithfield. Tyler rode forward with only one companion. He made similar demands to those granted to the Essex rebels, of which he may not have heard, but in addition to freedom for the peasants and the removal of all lordship except the King's, he also pressed for all church lands to be shared out to the peasants probably at Ball's suggestion. Taking a swig of beer, Tyler turned to remount his horse. As he did so, he touched his sword, and Walworth, the Lord Mayor of London, fearing an attack on the King, struck him dead. The rebels drew their bows for battle, and the King rode forward crying, "Would you shoot your king?". The rebels had never been against the King, and they let themselves be led away. Richard would not allow Walworth to attack them, though in the following weeks he retracted his concessions. The ring-leaders were rounded up and punished, and the lot of the peasant remained much the same.

**(Above) The Black Death resulted in harsh legislation by lords to hold on to scarce peasant labour.
(Right) Tyler is killed by Walworth, Mayor of London, while Richard II rides out to the rebels.**

Joan arriving to see
Charles VII, Chinon,
March 1429.

Joan of Arc
1412–31

*Joan of Arc was a peasant girl and
saint who revived French fortunes in
the Hundred Years War. She was
burned by the English as a witch.*

Joan was a shepherd girl living in Champagne in eastern France. At the age of 13 she first heard angel voices calling to her, and from then until the end of her life she claimed she was regularly visited by Saints Michael, Catherine and Margaret, the patron saints of France. Her voices directed her to go to the French King, Charles VII, and help him in his war with the English.

When she finally succeeded in 1429 in gaining admittance to the King's presence, he changed places with one of his courtiers, but she recognized the King immediately. Charles, his nobles and bishops were sceptical of the young girl's claim that she was sent to lead the French to victory. However, the situation was desperate; Charles had never been crowned, and had difficulty convincing himself, let alone the French people, that he was rightful king. Half of

France, including Paris, was occupied by the English, who claimed their king was king of France. The great city of Orléans had been besieged for many months.

In desperation, Joan was given her chance, equipped with man's armour and a sword found as she prophesied on the altar of a church. She wrought a miraculous change in French fortunes, leading the armies in person, and breathing courage into Charles and his soldiers. She raised the siege of Orléans, and destroyed the English reputation for invincibility.

In July 1429, Joan took Charles to Reims and saw him crowned. She kneeled before him and called him king for the first time. Joan was now the idol of France. She led the French against Paris, taunting the English openly to come out and fight her. The tide of war had changed, but Joan was captured by the Burgundians, allies of the English. In an attempt to escape, she jumped from a tower into a moat, but was knocked unconscious, and was lucky to be dragged out alive. The English bought her from her captors, and tried her for witchcraft, blasphemy, and "immodestly wearing men's clothes". She was burnt at the stake in Rouen on May 30 1431. She asked a monk to chant for her so

The execution of Joan of Arc.
The French King
subsequently reversed the
condemnation of witchcraft.
Joan's martyrdom only
increased her uplifting effect
on French morale.

she could hear heavenly words above the crackle of the flames. It was said that her heart was found intact in the ashes.

Joan's spirit lived on, and the French, with new national pride, defeated the English. Nearly 500 years later, in 1920, Joan of Arc was recognized as a saint by the Roman Catholic Church.

PRINTING

Johann Gutenberg
c.1400–68

William Caxton
c.1422–91

Johann Gutenberg began the age of printing, by constructing the first printing press, which began full-scale production in 1448. Gutenberg's great innovation was the use of movable and reusable metal type. William Caxton was the first man to set up a printing press in England, and was a pioneer of English-language publishing.

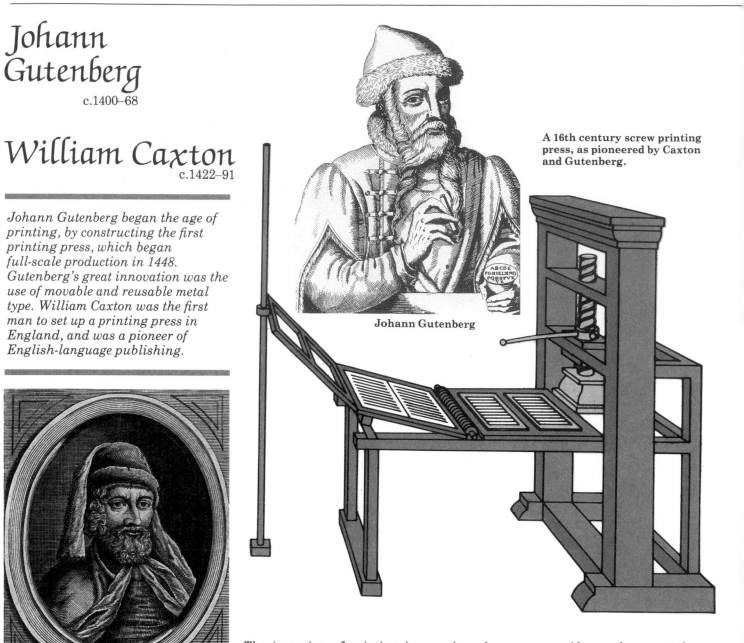

A 16th century screw printing press, as pioneered by Caxton and Gutenberg.

Johann Gutenberg

William Caxton

The invention of printing is a major landmark in the history of modern civilization. In the Middle Ages books were produced by hand ("manuscript"), painstakingly copied and illustrated ("illuminated"), usually by monks or priests. They were written in Latin. It was usually only those who were trained as churchmen who could read, together with a few aristocrats and occasionally a king. Only a few copies of each book would be in circulation. Printing dramatically changed this situation. Books became much more common, and therefore cheaper, and as a result, literacy became more widespread amongst those who were not churchmen. The possibility of producing thousands of pamphlets was a crucial factor in spreading the Reformation. Printing and cheap books meant scientific and other knowledge could be more widely known; Europeans were brought closer together.

The principle of printing using carved wooden blocks had been known to the Chinese since the 11th century, but it was in Europe that the crucial problem was solved of making individual letters (type) that could be moved but fitted securely and evenly in a frame. The

Gutenberg at work; a detail from Gutenberg's monument.

Frontispiece to Caxton's edition of the still popular *Fables of Aesop*.

man generally acknowledged to have achieved this first was Johann Gutenberg of Mainz in Germany. Gutenberg was a goldsmith, who spent 20 years secretly adapting methods used in making playing-cards and woodblock prints, and used his metalworking skills to cast letters to a uniform pattern. Others were experimenting in this at the same time, but it was Gutenberg who set up the first printing press to use movable type. To do this, Gutenberg borrowed money heavily from another goldsmith, Joachim Fust. By 1448, he had made enough type to print a whole Bible.

Gutenberg was no businessman, however, and in 1455, after a quarrel, Fust took possession of the house and press in payment of his debts. He continued to operate it, with his son-in-law, Peter Schöffer. Gutenberg started another press, on which in 1456 he printed the famous Gutenberg Bible (also known as the Mazarin Bible after the library where it was discovered). This is one of the oldest surviving printed books.

Gutenberg died in comparative poverty in 1468. In 1462 the city of Mainz was captured by enemies and sacked; printers from there fled to other cities throughout France and Germany, and the new invention was quickly spread. In 50 years printers were operating in 200 cities and towns in Europe.

The pioneering English printer was William Caxton. Caxton was a silk merchant, who lived in Bruges in Belgium from 1463 to 1469, and was a prominent member of the English trading community there. From 1471 to 1476, he was at the court of the English Duchess of Burgundy, one of the most magnificent courts in Europe. Like Gutenberg, he was interested in printing, but unlike the German he was wealthy, and possessed great talent for business. He learned printing in Cologne in Germany, and set up his first press in Bruges. There he produced the first printed book in English, his own translation from the French of *Recuyell of the Historyes of Troye*, about the ancient Trojan Wars. Caxton returned to England, and set up the first printing press at Westminster in London in 1476. In 1477, he published the first book in England, a translation by the King's father-in-law, Earl Rivers, *The Dictes and Sayengis of the Philosophers*.

Caxton attracted the interest and support of the wealthiest people in the land, including the royal family. Caxton published approximately 100 titles, of which copies of roughly one third survive. In addition to his own translations, he printed the works of the English poets Geoffrey Chaucer and John Gower, and author Thomas Malory, and played a key role in the first great age of English literature.

One of the results of printing was the spread and development of European languages other than Latin, and for none was this more true than English, which began to develop as a recognizable national language, rather than simply a collection of regional dialects.

Christopher Columbus

1451–1506

Christopher Columbus was an Italian explorer, who in 1492 discovered America. He made four voyages to America under the Spanish flag between 1492 and 1504.

Columbus was the son of a weaver in the port of Genoa. He trained as a wool-comber, but was attracted to the sea, and at 14 ran away to become a sailor. After some years at sea, he was shipwrecked when his ship caught fire off the coast of Portugal, and he was forced to swim ashore on a plank. He settled in Portugal, married, and became a mapmaker.

Portugal was the greatest seafaring nation of the 15th century, under the encouragement of Prince Henry the Navigator (1394–1460), and it was not

(below left) Contemporary engravings of Columbus's first landing on Hispaniola.

(bottom right) Columbus received by his patrons, King Ferdinand and Queen Isabella of Spain.

(right, map) The four voyages of Columbus to the New World.

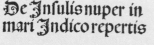

De Insulis nuper in mari Indico repertis

First Voyage 1492-3

Second voyage 1493-6

Fourth voyage 1502-3

Third voyage 1498

long before Columbus was bitten by the desire to return to sea. He conceived an ambitious plan. There was a rich trade at this time in spices, silks and other luxuries from China and India in the East. Columbus shared the belief that was becoming widespread amongst navigators that the world was round. He thought it would therefore be possible to reach the East by sailing west. He believed this would cut the journey time, as no one at that time knew how large the world really was. He took his plan to the Kings of Portugal, England and Spain, but none of them was interested in such a speculative enterprise.

Columbus spent many fruitless and frustrating years at various courts, dismissed as impractical or just insane. It was a piece of luck that finally brought Columbus his reward. On the way from the Spanish court to the French, he

stopped at a monastery, where he had left his son. He told the monks his ideas, and the abbot, who was formerly Queen Isabella's confessor, wrote to the Queen on his behalf, and at last won him a favourable audience. Thus it was that on August 3 1492 this Genoese sailor set off from Palos in Southern Spain under the colours of the King and Queen of Spain, Ferdinand and Isabella. He had been promised the Governorship of any lands he discovered, and a proportion of the profits. He took 3 tiny ships, the *Santa Maria, Pinta* and *Niña*, and 87 men, many of whom had been recruited from prisons.

After stopping in the Canary Islands to refit, Columbus headed out into the "Sea of Darkness" as it was known. Portuguese sailors had sailed right down the coast of Africa, but no one had dared to venture out into the Atlantic Ocean. To superstitious sailors it was the domain of sea monsters, with the perpetual risk of sailing over the edge of the world. As they sailed further, with no sight of land, so they became more restless. Eventually Columbus was threatened with open mutiny. Columbus changed his logbook entries to make it seem they were nearer home than they were, and promised to turn back in three days if land was not sighted.

By that time, there were signs that land was near; branches floating by, and birds that were land not sea birds. At two in the morning on October 12, 1492, land was sighted; Watling Island in the Bahamas, which Columbus named San Salvador. European eyes looked on America for the first time since the Vikings had done so (and long been forgotten) 500 years earlier. Cuba and Hispaniola (Haiti) were also discovered, and 39 men were left on Hispaniola, with supplies. Columbus returned home with his two remaining ships (*Santa Maria* was wrecked), six captives and strange animals and flowers. Columbus was convinced he had reached Asia. He was feted as a hero

Columbus made three more voyages. The second aimed at truly colonising the new land, and converting the natives to Christianity. Leaving in September 1493 he took more than 1,000 men, in 17 ships. He discovered Guadelupe, Puerto Rico and Jamaica, and though his colonists on Hispaniola had been massacred by Indians, he founded the city of Isabella there, the first European city in the "New World".

On his third voyage, Columbus explored the mainland of South America, which he thought was another island, and Trinidad. Columbus had many rivals at the Spanish court, and reports of rebellion on Hispaniola caused Ferdinand and Isabella to send out a new Governor, Francisco de Bobadilla. Columbus resisted him, and was returned to Spain in 1500 in chains.

With difficulty, Columbus regained royal favour, but his fourth voyage (1502–04) was disastrous. He explored Honduras, Nicaragua and Panama, but he suffered mutinies and shipwreck. He returned empty-handed to Spain with one vessel, to find his patron the Queen had died. He had failed to find a route to the Indies to match the one just opened by Vasco da Gama, a Portuguese who sailed round Africa. He spend the final two years of his life pleading with the King for the rewards he had been promised from his first voyage. He died in poverty. He still believed he had landed in Asia, and was never to know that his real achievement, for which he will always be remembered, was the discovery of a continent.

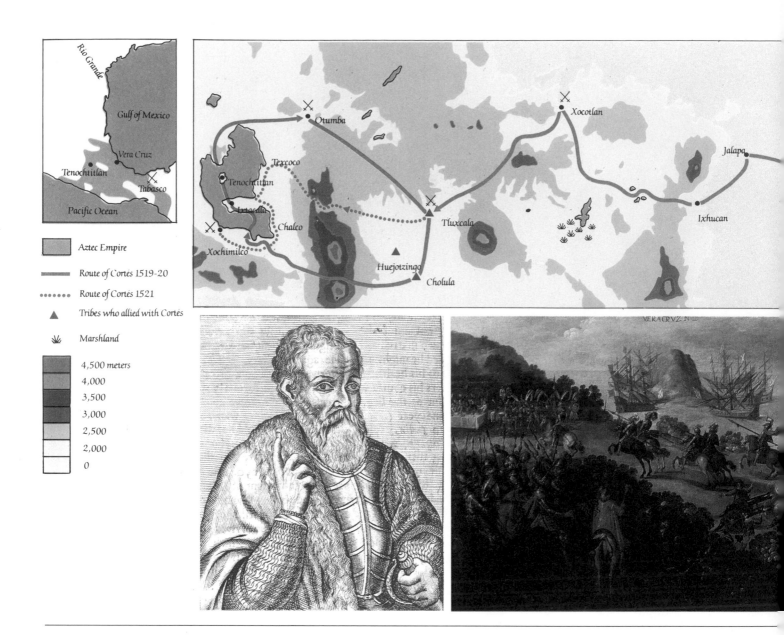

Hernándo Cortés

1485–1547

Cortés was a Spanish adventurer and explorer, who conquered Mexico from the Aztecs. He also discovered Lower California.

Cortés has gone down in history as the destroyer of a civilization, that of the Aztecs, and his cruelty has tended to have been remembered more than his bravery. He was typical of the Spanish *conquistadores*; bold and restless men who explored unknown parts of the New World at great risk, in search of heroic adventure, but also to add to their own wealth.

Cortés came originally from Salamanca in Spain, but when he was forced by his father to study law, he ran away to Hispaniola (Haiti). He served with Velázquez, Governor of Cuba, and in 1518, he was sent to explore the American mainland. He took 600 volunteers in 11 ships. The town of Vera Cruz was founded, and Cortés was elected Captain-General by the citizens (his crew), giving him independence from Velázquez.

Cortés marched inland to the magnificent city of Tenochtitlán, capital of the Aztec Empire. He was welcomed by the emperor, Montezuma, who believed that he was Quetzalcoatl, a god believed to have been fair-skinned like the Europeans. Cortés imprisoned Montezuma, intending to rule through him and convert the Aztecs to Christianity.

Velázquez sent an army, angered by Cortés disobedience, and Cortés had to march out to meet it. He persuaded it to join him, but on returning to Tenochtitlán found that the Aztecs had risen and killed Montezuma. After desperate fighting, Cortés recaptured the city in 1521. In 1522 he was appointed Captain-General of "New Spain" as it was called, by King Charles of Spain. He rebuilt the city, now Mexico City, in Spanish style. His rule over the Aztecs was not unjust, and his reputation for cruelty was not

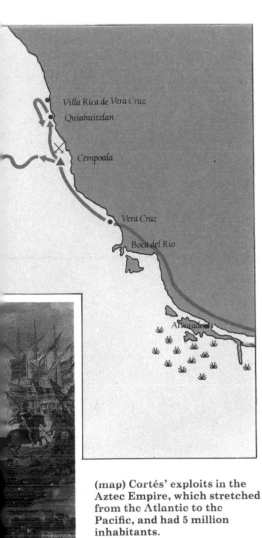

(map) Cortés' exploits in the Aztec Empire, which stretched from the Atlantic to the Pacific, and had 5 million inhabitants.

(left) Cortés lands at Vera Cruz. The ships were destroyed to prevent anyone turning back.

fully warranted.

Charles was distrustful of the *conquistadores* and the way they were carving out large personal estates. Cortés, despite pleading his case in Spain, from 1528 to 1530, was made merely military commander, with political control passing to a Governor-General. He led expeditions to the Pacific coast, and claimed Lower California for Spain in 1533, but received scant recognition when he returned to Spain. On one occasion he told Charles he was the man who had gained him more provinces than his father left him towns, but the king, having gained enormously by his conquests, had no further use for him, and Cortés died in poverty.

Suleiman the Magnificent
1494–1566

Suleiman the Magnificent was Sultan of Turkey, 1520–66. Under him, the empire of the Ottoman Turks reached its peak.

As a result of the Mongol advances under Genghis, the Turks had moved from their home in Turkestan in central Asia at the end of the 13th century into the decaying Eastern Roman Empire. Under Suleiman's grandfather Mohammed the Conqueror, they captured the capital Constantinople (renamed Istanbul) in 1453. Mohammed conquered 12 kingdoms and 200 cities. His son Selim the Grim added Syria, Egypt, and Arabia.

Suleiman inherited this great empire in 1520, and was determined to continue his father's conquests. In 1521 he captured Belgrade, and in 1526 defeated and killed King Lewis II of Hungary at the battle of Mohacs. By 1540, most of Hungary had been brought under Turkish rule. Suleiman menaced Austria, and he successfully held off attacks from Ferdinand, Duke of Austria. He made alliance with Francis I, King of France, who was at war with Ferdinand's brother, the Emperor Charles V.

Suleiman's fleet was commanded by the pirate ruler of Algiers, Kair ad-Din, known as Barbarossa (Redbeard), who attacked shipping and ravaged the coasts of Italy and Spain using a French port as his winter base. In the East, Suleiman extended his rule as far as Baghdad.

Suleiman was proud and aggressive, but also artistic and well-read. He constructed new mosques, roads and bridges, codified laws, and patronized the arts. While aiming to conquer the world, he did not forcibly convert his subjects to Islam, with one exception. The Ottoman army and civil service was largely made up of slaves. Many of these were the products of a regular levy of Christian boys. These boys were brought up as Muslims, and formed the backbone

The conquests of Suleiman the Magnificent.

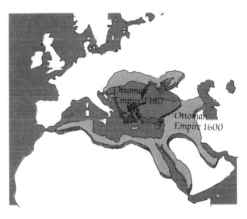

of the government, fanatically loyal to the sultan. They could rise high in the government if talented, and even marry into the sultan's family, although they still remained slaves.

There was no fixed law of succession, and it was usual for sultans to kill most of their close relatives, to remove rivals. Suleiman had his eldest son Mustafa strangled in 1553, and another son executed in 1561. He died in battle in Hungary, and after him the Ottoman Empire, which depended very much on the capabilities of its ruler, began a long slow decline.

THE REFORMATION

Martin Luther
1483–1546

John Calvin
1509–1564

Luther was a German religious reformer and mystic, whose attack on what he saw as the corruption and decadence of the Roman Catholic Church initiated the Reformation. Calvin was the great organiser and theologian of the Protestant movement that Luther began, and the father of what became known in England as Puritanism.

Calvin returns to Geneva after three years exile in Strasbourg (1541).

At the start of the 16th century, all Christian people of western and central Europe were members of the Roman Catholic Church, headed by the pope in Rome. Popular religion had developed many superstitions that had no place in the teaching of the early Church fathers. The popes were more like Italian princes than religious leaders. The Reformation was a movement that grew up in the 16th century to correct these corruptions.

It was all started by Luther. He was the son of a miner, and a brilliant scholar. After being struck by lightning, he took a vow that he would become a monk. Luther was subject to fits of black depression, when he despaired of salvation. All the set procedures of the Church could not erase his feeling of unworthiness and sin. It was while reading St. Paul's letter to the Romans, that the answer came. Luther came to believe that man is saved from his sin only by his faith in Christ. Merely doing good works, the Church's remedy, was useless.

Luther was led on to question many of the Church's practices and ceremonies, which had brought him no satisfaction, and claimed they had no basis in the Bible. Luther wrote his conclusions in *95 Theses*, and nailed them to the door of Wittenberg Cathedral. Through the new medium of printing, they were rapidly circulated throughout Europe and struck a response from many religious-minded people concerned at the state of the Church.

Luther followed up the *95 Theses* with many pamphlets and books. He denied the pope's claim to absolute authority, and attacked the wealth and corruption of the Church, and the special place of priests in society. He proclaimed a "priesthood of all believers". Faith was the key, not observance of ceremonies. The role of priests (now called ministers) was simply to preach the word of God. They were free to marry; Luther himself ceased to be a monk, and married a former nun. Monasteries, which often had great wealth, were not necessary. Luther particularly attacked "indulgences"; documents sold by the Church which were supposed to bring admittance to heaven in return for payment of money.

Calvin preaching in Geneva. To Calvin, preaching was a minister's most important occupation. (Map) The spread of Protestantism, 1520–60.

Luther was excommunicated by the Pope, and outlawed by the Holy Roman Emperor. When called upon to recant, he said, "Here I stand. I can do no other, so help me God." He was protected by Duke Frederick the Wise of Saxony, who adopted Luther's ideas. Luther was able to continue attacking the Catholic Church free from persecution. The split between Catholics and Protestants, as the followers of Luther and other reformers were known, became permanent.

The greatest of these other reformers, and the one who left the strongest mark on the future shape of the Reformed churches was the Frenchman, John Calvin. Calvin was trained as a lawyer, and brought to the Reformation a harshly logical and ordered mind, allied with great learning and a severe sense of morality.

Calvin had been converted to reformed doctrines by 1533, and had been forced to flee France for fear of persecution. In 1536 he first published *The Institutes of the Christian Religion*, the most systematic exposition of the Reformed faith. Calvin stopped in Geneva, which was in the process of asserting its independence from its bishop overlord, and was invited by the reforming preacher, Guillaume Farel, to stay and help organize the new church

there. Calvin accepted the position and under his leadership, Geneva became known as the "Protestant Rome".

At first Calvin found opposition from the city authorities who were anxious to assert their control over all affairs in the city previously under the bishop's authority, while Calvin believed ministers should exercise authority even over non-religious matters. In 1538, the opposition forced Calvin to leave Geneva, and until 1541 he lived in Strasbourg. While he was there he married. In 1541, Calvin's supporters gained the ascendancy in Geneva, and he was invited back. In the next few years, he gained control of all aspects of life in the city-state.

Calvin's view of Christianity and church government derived from his conclusion from his reading of the Bible that the faithful were chosen by God before creation (predestination of the elect). The church is the organisation of the elect, and has no place for the corrupt. The ministers exercised control over all aspects of people's behaviour, with the power to excommunicate or even execute. All were compelled to go to church on Sundays, rich clothes and jewellery were forbidden, and citizens were encouraged to keep a watch over each other for any heresy or immorality.

Calvinism spread quickly. Calvin's fol-

lowers were called Puritans in England, while in Scotland and America, they were known as Presbyterians. The majority of French protestants (Huguenots) were Calvinists. The Calvinists' great strength was their tightly-knit discipline, independent of any other church, and the conviction that they were the chosen ones of God. This led them to become involved in many political resistance movements against "ungodly rulers", especially in England, France and Holland.

39

Henry VIII
1491–1547

King Henry VIII ruled England from 1509 to 1547. His reign saw the Dissolution of the Monasteries and the separation of the Church of England from Roman Catholicism. He increased the prestige of the Crown, and the power of Parliament, which he used to extend his power.

King Henry VIII was the second son of Henry VII. It was intended that he should become a priest, which was usual for the younger sons of nobles in those days, but his elder brother died, and in 1509, at the age of 18, he succeeded his father as king. He immediately married his brother's widow, the Spanish princess, Catherine of Aragon.

In his youth, Henry was many people's ideal of a king, and this did much to raise the popularity of the monarchy. He was tall and handsome, enjoying sports, dancing, hunting and fighting, but was also a scholar. He received from the pope the title "Defender of the Faith" which English monarchs still bear, for writing a book defending the Church.

Henry was also a vain man, and found a rival in Francis I, the young king of France. This resulted in sporadic fighting between England and France, as well as extravagant one-upmanship. The most famous example was when they met each other in 1520, when their pavilions were so sumptuous it seemed to be a "field of cloth of gold", Henry once astonished and embarrassed the French Ambassador by rolling down his stocking and asking the Frenchman if his master could boast of such a finely shaped leg!

For much of his youth. Henry left the serious government of the country to Cardinal Wolsey, the leader of the Roman Catholic Church in England, and Thomas More, a lawyer and accomplished scholar. Wolsey, the son of a butcher, became rich in the King's service, and built himself the palace at Hampton Court. Henry was ruthless in removing his advisors when they did not satisfy him, and Wolsey lost the king's favour when he was unable to obtain permission from the Pope for Henry to divorce his wife. This had become the King's greatest desire, for he wanted a son to succeed him, and Catherine had only borne a daughter, Mary, and was too old to have more children.

Unable to obtain satisfaction from the Pope, Henry went ahead on his own. He declared by Act of Parliament that he, not the Pope, was head of the Church in England. In January 1533 he married Anne Boleyn, though his marriage to Catherine was not annulled until May, by Thomas Cranmer, whom Henry appointed Archbishop of Canterbury. Anne too failed to bear a son, her only child being Elizabeth, and in 1536 she was beheaded so that Henry could marry Jane Seymour, who did have a son, Edward, but died in childbirth.

The King's new advisor was Thomas Cromwell, who carried out reforms of religion and government. Thomas More refused to accept that the king could be

head of the Church, and was executed. The great Roman Catholic monasteries, some of which were very rich, were dissolved by Act of Parliament, bringing the Crown a great deal of money. This caused unrest in the countryside, and a revolt broke out in Yorkshire called the "Pilgrimage of Grace", which was violently put down.

Henry became very fat as he grew older. Special machinery had to be made to lower him onto his horse, and to carry him upstairs! Sometimes described as a tyrant, Henry was a strong ruler, who insisted on his will being followed, even when he suddenly changed his mind. To make England more effective in war, he expanded the English Navy, building ships like the *Mary Rose*, named after his daughter, and the *Great Harry*, and thus began the great age of English seafaring. He left behind him a united kingdom, though one which had undergone many changes, especially religious, and a popular monarchy that was to reach its high point under his daughter, Elizabeth.

(Left) The Great Hall at Hampton Court.
(Below) Jousts at Westminster Abbey, 1510. Jousting was one of Henry's favourite sports, until an ulcer on his leg prevented him taking part. Lack of exercise then caused him to become very overweight.
(Bottom left) Henry VIII takes ship at Dover, 1520.
(Bottom right) The meeting with Francis I on the Field of Cloth of Gold.

Thomas Cranmer
1489–1556

Thomas Cranmer, Archbishop of Canterbury, directed the English Reformation for Henry VIII. He was one of the first Anglican martyrs.

Cranmer was a studious, retiring academic, who first came to the King's attention when he was seeking the approval of European universities for the annulment of his marriage to Catherine of Aragon. Cranmer, chaplain to Anne Boleyn's father, went on a mission to Italy for this purpose. He very reluctantly accepted the King's appointment of him as Archbishop in 1533.

Cranmer's deepest belief was in the supremacy of royal authority. This made him a compliant servant of the King's policy, and he organized the King's divorces and marriages. As a Protestant, he approved of the Dissolution of the Monasteries. Cranmer married twice, in 1515, and 1532. The King disapproved of married clergy, and this was forbidden in 1539. Cranmer had to keep his wife hidden, secreting her in a wardrobe when he moved house. Henry had considerable affection for Cranmer, and Cranmer's enemies amongst the more conservative courtiers were unable to discredit him.

Cranmer, though a willing servant of any royal whim, was not simply a place-seeker. He composed the new litany for the Church of England, and in the reign of Henry's son Edward VI wrote the new prayer-book. This remained in use for 400 years, virtually unchanged. In these religious works, Cranmer is revealed as a highly gifted writer, with great poetic ability. His skillful amalgamation of different strands of Christian practice produced a Church service that all but extremists could accept. Cranmer placed English Bibles in all churches, spreading the Protestant faith.

There can be no doubt of the sincerity of Cranmer's belief, but in the reign of Mary he was faced with an awful dilemma. As a believer in the divine authority of kings, he had signed Edward VI's will making Jane Grey successor. When Edward died in 1553, Mary easily defeated Jane, and Cranmer was arrested for treason. She demanded he recant his Protestantism. All his life he had obeyed the monarch. Eventually he agreed to do so. However, at the ceremony in Oxford, where he was to make this public, he withdrew his recantation. On the same day (March 21 1556) he died a martyr's death at the stake. He thrust the hand that had signed the recantation first into the flames, saying, "this hath offended", and perished a hero.

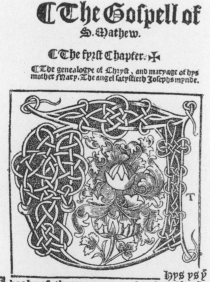

Page from Cranmer's translation of the Bible, 1540.

Mary I
1516–58

Mary I reigned as Queen of England 1553–58. She restored the Roman Catholic faith, and executed some 300 Protestants, earning herself the name 'Bloody Mary'. She also made an unpopular Spanish alliance, and lost Calais, England's last possession in France.

Mary was the only surviving child of Cathcrine of Aragon's marriage to Henry VIII, and remained loyal to her mother's Catholic faith. After her mother's marriage was annulled. Mary was declared illegitimate. She was put under great pressure to renounce Catholicism, and eventually acknowledged the Royal Headship of the Church, and her own illegitimacy. She was given a place in the succession after the legitimate offspring. She immediately sought secret forgiveness from the Pope. During Edward VI's reign (1547–53), she maintained her Catholic faith. When Edward died, aged 16, a faction tried to make Jane Grey queen, to preserve a Protestant monarchy. Mary was a popular figure, and as the eldest surviving child of Henry VIII, the obvious successor. She easily defeated her rival, and became queen with the support of the great majority of her subjects.

She soon forfeited this popularity, however. She shared none of the practicality of her father or sister, Elizabeth, but had an overriding sense of duty to her faith, and love for her mother's country, Spain. She married King Philip II of Spain, and the English people had a great dislike of being ruled by a foreigner, and feared being involved in Spain's war with France. This eventually happened, and England lost Calais. Mary declared that when she died, Calais would be found engraved on her heart. Parliament refused to make Philip king.

Mary's greatest error, however was her handling of the religious issue. The English were by no means averse to a

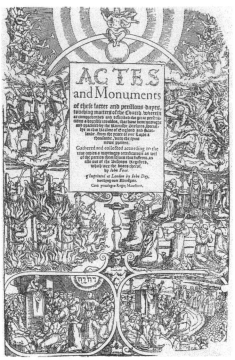

Title page of *Actes and Monuments*
(1563), describing Mary's persecutions. It
was a popular book in Elizabeth's reign.

Tortures like the rack were used to
extract recantations from Protestants.

return to the kind of "Catholicism
without the pope" practised in Henry
VIII's last years. Mary went much
further, however, under the influence of
Cardinal Pole, and against the warnings
of Philip. In 1554, Mary, Philip, and
Parliament knelt while Pole gave them
absolution and welcomed them back
under papal authority. Mary dismissed
some 2,000 married clergy. She revived
the heresy laws, and 300 were burned
at the stake, including Cranmer, and
Bishops Latimer and Ridley. About 800
fled to Calvinist strongholds in Europe.

The number of executions was by no
means high compared to what was done
in Europe at this time, but quite
contrary to English practice. To Englishmen ever since, Mary has been
"Bloody Mary". To Mary's despair she
died childless, leaving England to the
Protestant Elizabeth.

The Spanish Armada, 1588. Many Spanish galleons were lost in storms on the return journey round the north of Scotland.

(Inset right) Shakespeare's Globe theatre. London theatres and bear-gardens were on the south bank of the Thames, outside the City.

An Elizabethan courtier, possibly Essex.

Elizabeth I
1533–1603

Queen of England from 1558–1603, Elizabeth inspired a period of exploration and adventure, and a flowering of the arts. There was war with Spain from 1585 to 1603.

Queen Elizabeth was the daughter of Henry VIII and Anne Boleyn. She was only two years old when her mother was beheaded. She was regarded as illegitimate until her father's last will placed her third in succession behind her half-brother Edward and her half-sister Mary. She survived the short reigns of both, though under the Catholic Mary she was regarded with suspicion as the Protestant heiress. She spent two months in the Tower as a result.

Elizabeth was 25 years old when she succeeded on the death of her sister. She inherited characteristics from both her father and her grandfather Henry VII. Like Henry VIII she was tall and red-headed, strong-willed and tough, but liable to unpredictable changes of mind.

From her grandfather she inherited a great deal of political cunning and patience, as well as a trace of meanness. She was well-fitted to be a queen. She had a great ability to command her subjects' loyalty and even love. She had consummate skill as a parliamentary manager: a new requirement for an English monarch, but one in which her successors James I and Charles I were disastrously deficient. This had become important because of the role Parliament had been given in Henry VIII's reign, and because the Crown was usually short of money. Only Parliament could approve taxes to relieve that shortage.

There were two main bones of contention between Parliament and the Queen: her marriage, and the Church. Elizabeth never married, preferring to preserve her independence. The Protestant House of Commons was concerned that she should produce an heir, for if she did not do so her successor would be the Catholic Mary, Queen of Scots (until Mary's death in 1587). Elizabeth preferred to remain the "virgin queen", though she had a number of favourites, notably the Earls of Leicester and Essex. She used

the subject as an instrument of diplomacy to save England from a coalition of the Catholic powers, holding open the prospect of marriage to Philip of Spain, her sister's widower, and then to the French prince Francis, Duke of Alençon. Probably she never intended to marry any of them. She regarded her marriage as none of Parliament's business, and skillfully avoided discussing the subject while at the same time retaining their goodwill.

Elizabeth was indifferent to the religious issues of the time, unlike Parliament and many of her close advisors who were Calvinist Puritans, and wanted a Church with no bishops or ceremonial. Elizabeth most of all wanted a Church that the majority of her subjects would accept. This she achieved, despite opposition from Puritan and Catholic extremists. She disclaimed any desire to look into men's souls, and was concerned only with outward loyalty. She only allowed persecution of Catholics after the Pope declared her deposed and being a Catholic meant supporting her overthrow.

Under Elizabeth a new sense of national identity grew up. It inspired the semi-piratical activities of Drake and others in their attacks on Spanish property in America, as well as more legitimate activities. It was closely identified with the person of the Queen, and grew into the cult of "Gloriana", another name for the Queen. This was fueled by Elizabeth herself, most notably when the Spanish Armada was approaching in 1588. She rode out on a white horse to see her troops at Tilbury near London, and declared to them that though she had the body of a "weak and feeble woman," she had the heart of a king, and a king of England too.

This spirit found expression in great voyages of trade and discovery to America, Russia and other places, and the start of colonization in Virginia (named after the Queen). The growth of prosperity and peace in England encouraged the growth of the arts, particularly poetry and the theatre. The greatest exponent of both of these was William Shakespeare, in whose works the English language reached a new level of poetry.

Elizabeth's reign also however saw much poverty, and an effort was made to deal with this in poor relief measures, that were to last unchanged until 1834. The Crown itself was perpetually short of money. This led the Queen to encourage Drake and Hawkins' attacks on the Spanish Main (the waters around America which Spain claimed as its own), sharing in the profits. It also meant she was always travelling from place to place and scrounging hospitality from her subjects; many houses could claim "Queen Elizabeth slept here".

Sir Francis Drake

c.1543–1596

Sir Francis Drake was the first Englishman to sail round the world. He captured large amounts of treasure in raids on the Spanish in the New World, and was Vice-Admiral in the fight against the Spanish Armada.

In Drake's time, Catholic Spain and Portugal regarded America as their private preserve; Drake, and other "sea-dogs" like Sir Richard Grenville and Sir John Hawkins were determined to put an end to that. Drake was an inspiring leader, a fanatical Protestant and patriot as well as an original tactician.

During the 1570s, Drake built a reputation as the most daring privateer on the Spanish Main. His greatest success was in 1572, when he ambushed the mule train carrying silver to the port of Nombre de Dios in Panama. During this expedition he caught his first sight of the Pacific, and prayed that one day he would sail an English ship on those waters.

His prayer came true in 1578. Drake set out in 1577 with four ships. His flagship was *Pelican*, soon changed to *Golden Hind*, after the crest of Sir Christopher Hatton, one of the sponsors. Only Drake's ship made it round the southern tip of South America; the others were sunk or turned back. He raided Spanish ships and ports in the Pacific, and claimed California for the Queen, naming it New Albion. Fearing the Spaniards would ambush him, he decided to cross the Pacific. He sailed home via the Moluccas and Java, picking up valuable spices, and returned to England round the Cape of Good Hope. The Queen knighted Drake on the deck of *Golden Hind* on his arrival in September 1580. The voyage produced a profit of 4,700 percent. The Queen's share was £160,000.

War with Spain officially broke out in 1585. Drake's greatest contribution was a daring raid on the port of Cádiz. By the use of fire-ships, he destroyed a large part of the invasion fleet, the Armada. This delayed its sailing for a crucial year. This became known as "singeing the King of Spain's beard".

When the Armada came, in 1588, Drake was English second-in-command. The legend that he finished a game of bowls before taking to sea against the approaching invader first grew up a century later, and is unlike the fiery and warlike Drake. He played a leading part in the battle, in which the smaller English ships harassed the Spanish galleons to defeat: a defeat which turned into a rout when the wind scattered the Spaniards, and forced them to try to return home round the north of Scotland. Many were wrecked in the attempt.

Drake died of dysentery in 1596, while on another raid in the West Indies. He left behind him a reputation that was to inspire generations of English seafarers.

Legend

Hapsburg Empire
Under English control
-- Armada route
Engagement zone
Spanish ships
English ships
Wind direction
Current
/// Sandbanks

(Right) While the Spanish demanded Drake be punished for piracy, Elizabeth showed her approval by knighting him on the deck of his ship.

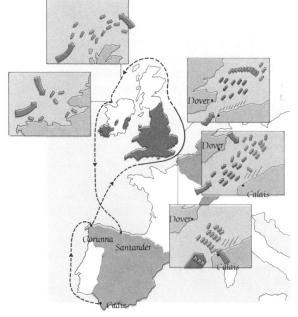

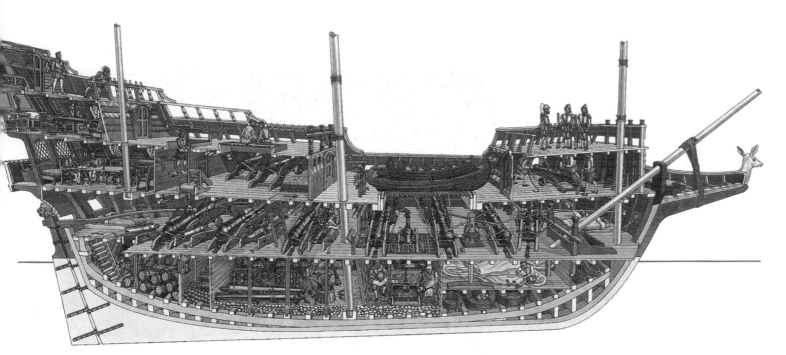

Sir Walter Raleigh

c.1552–1618

Sir Walter Raleigh was a soldier, courtier, writer and explorer of the great Elizabethan age. He was an early pioneer of the colonization of North America.

(Above) *Golden Hind*
(Below) Raleigh's servant, seeing him smoking, throws water on him, believing he is on fire.

Raleigh was a many-sided man, typical of the adventurous spirits of Elizabeth I's England. Born in Devon, he distinguished himself fighting rebels in Ireland in 1580, and this brought him to the attention of the Queen.

At Court, Raleigh's charm, good looks and rich clothes made him a favourite of the Queen. A popular story has him laying his costly cloak courteously over a muddy spot so that the Queen should not get her feet wet. He was also a proud, impatient man, and aroused many enemies. The Queen gave him the nickname 'Water', perhaps showing she was aware of the instability of his character. She lavished favours on him, however, giving him lucrative offices, estates in Ireland, and knighting him in 1585.

He fell from favour in 1592, when his secret marriage to one of Elizabeth's Maids of Honour roused the Queen's jealousy. He and his wife were imprisoned in the Tower for a time, and

Raleigh never fully regained favour.

Raleigh was a man of vision, but was often unable to make his ideas work. In 1584–89 he tried to establish a colony on Roanoke Island (in present day North Carolina). He called this Virginia in honour of the "virgin queen", but the enterprise failed. He did introduce into England two crops discovered in America; potatoes and tobacco. He caused an immense stir when he first appeared at Court surrounded in smoke from his pipe.

In 1595 he led an expedition to Guyana, in search of the fabled city of gold, 'El Dorado'. He found no gold, but explored 3,000 miles (4,830 km) of the Orinoco valley.

His fortunes changed under James I, and in 1603 he was arrested on a charge of treason. He conducted his trial so well that he recovered his popularity. He was still sentenced to death, only to be reprieved on the scaffold. He was held in the Tower until 1616, spending his time writing a history of the world. He was released to go on another expedition to find gold but this failed. Against his order, his men attacked a Spanish settlement. He had been strictly ordered by the King not to interfere with Spain, and on his return, this spectacular, but ultimately tragic figure, was executed. He faced death with courage, saying of the axe, "This is sharp medicine; but it is a sure cure for all diseases".

Mary, Queen of Scots
1542–87

Mary Stuart was Queen of Scotland, 1542–67 and of France, 1559–60. She was executed in England in 1587.

Henry, Lord Darnley, Mary's second husband.

Mary, Queen of Scots has been seen as one of the most tragic and romantic figures in British history. Her story is a sad one, though one in which she was not always the innocent victim. She became queen when seven days old on the death of her father James V. She was engaged to the son of the French King to cement the traditional Franco-Scottish alliance, and was taken to France where she was educated. She married in 1558, and in 1559 her husband became King Francis II but she was Queen of France for barely a year before her young husband died.

Mary was forced to return to Scotland, a country of which she knew little. Her French manners and Catholicism were out of place in Scotland, which had become largely Protestant. She insisted on tolerance towards Catholics, earning her the enmity of the fiery Scots preacher, John Knox. Mary had brains and charm, but was ruled by her passions, and by her ambition for the English Crown. Mary was cousin of Queen Elizabeth of England, and her heir so long as Elizabeth did not have a child. Since the death of Mary I in 1558, Mary had called herself Queen of England. To strengthen her claim, she married her cousin Henry Stuart, Lord Darnley, who also had English royal blood, in 1565.

Mary refused, however, to give Darnley any right to the Scottish throne, on the advice of David Rizzio, her arrogant Italian secretary and musician. Darnley, a weak and vain man, became jealous of Rizzio, and on March 9 1566 had him murdered in her presence. He received 56 stab wounds. Mary was pregnant at the time, and soon after her son, James, was born, she had her revenge. She pretended to pardon the murderers, and flattered Darnley into reconciliation. When Darnley became ill with smallpox, she induced him to live in a house at Kirk o'Field near Edinburgh. One night the house was blown up; Darnley's body was discovered nearby, strangled and unburned. Three months later Mary married the Earl of Bothwell, who was suspected of being responsible for Darnley's murder.

The scandal that arose brought the Protestant nobles into open revolt. Mary was made to abdicate. Her infant son became James VI (later James I of England). She was imprisoned in a castle on Loch Leven. Aided by friendly servants, she escaped by boat in May 1568. She raised an army, but was defeated and crossed into England, throwing herself on the mercy of her cousin.

The arrival of someone claiming to be Queen of England presented Elizabeth with a great dilemma. Executing a fellow-queen was repugnant to her, and as a kinswoman, Mary merited protection. On the other hand, Mary was the heir to the throne, and when the Pope excommunicated Elizabeth in 1570, was regarded by many Catholics as the rightful queen. Her presence was the focus for plots to depose Elizabeth, and an encouragement to France to invade in her aid. Elizabeth's ministers urged her to have Mary executed. Elizabeth would not do so, resting content with keepng her locked away. For Elizabeth, Mary served a useful purpose of discouraging Philip of Spain from trying to depose her, when doing so would place the pro-French Mary on the throne.

Elizabeth therefore kept her cousin alive. A number of plots (Ridolfi plot 1571–72, Throckmorton plot 1582) to release her and make her queen were exposed; each time Elizabeth resisted her ministers' claims that Mary herself was involved. She had much sympathy for Mary, and her hard life, calling her the "daughter of debate". Finally she was convinced by evidence produced by her secret service, that Mary was involved in the Babington plot of 1586, and reluctantly agreed to her execution. The sad, but still beautiful Mary Stuart was beheaded at Fotheringay Castle on February 8 1587. Her last words, given to her ladies-in-waiting, were "cease to lament, for you shall now see a final end to Mary Stuart's troubles. I pray you take this message when you go; that I die true to my religion, to Scotland and to France".

(Above) Mary's bitter enemy, John Knox, the Scottish Calvinist preacher. Knox harangued Mary to her face for her Catholicism, and strongly criticised the rule of women.

(Below) Mary prepares for her death in Fotheringay Castle, February 8 1587.

Mary returning to Scotland after the death of her first husband, Francis II of France. She loved France, and was reluctant to leave it for Scotland, a land she barely knew.

Guy Fawkes
1570–1606

Guy Fawkes was one of the conspirators in the plan to blow up the English Houses of Parliament and kill King James I in 1605, known as the Gunpowder Plot. Fawkes was the member of the group who was actually discovered with the barrels of gunpowder on November 5 1605.

CONCILVM SEP-TEM NOBILIVM ANGLORVM CONIVRANTIVM IN NECEM IACOB
MAGNÆ BRITANNIÆ REGIS TOTIVSQ ANGLICI CONVOCATI PARLEMENTI.

James I was the son of Mary, Queen of Scots, and in 1603 succeeded his cousin, Queen Elizabeth, on the throne of England. The son of a Catholic, James was brought up as a Protestant. When he became king, both Puritans and Catholics expected his religious policy to favour them. In fact, James maintained Elizabeth's Church of England, and a number of English Catholics resolved to kill him. They decided to do this at the opening of Parliament in November

(Top right) The Conspirators.
(Below) A Royalist engraving shows the "eye of God" spying Fawkes on the way to the Houses of Parliament.

Gun Powder Treafon.

1605, so that the King, Queen, Prince of Wales and the Protestant House of Commons would all be destroyed. Simultaneously they planned a rising in the Midlands to place Prince Charles, the king's second son, on the throne.

The leader of the conspiracy was Robert Catesby, a zealous Catholic and a strong leader. The first conspirators were his cousin Thomas Winter, Thomas Percy, John Wright and Guy Fawkes. Fawkes was a Yorkshire gentleman and a fanatical convert to Catholicism. He had served during the 1590s with the Spanish army against Protestants in the Netherlands, a time when Spain was at war with England.

The plotters hired a house next to the Parliament buildings in May 1604, and dug a passage under the House of Lords from its cellar. In March 1605, they were able to rent the cellar directly under the Palace of Westminster, and joined the two. Fawkes arranged the storage of 20 barrels of gunpowder there, with iron bars on top for greater impact. They were hidden beneath firewood and coal and tended by Fawkes under the name of John Johnson.

More conspirators had been introduced, and one, Francis Tresham, gave the plot away by sending a warning to his cousin, Lord Monteagle, to stay away from Parliament. Monteagle showed the note to Lord Salisbury, the king's chief minister, and on November 4 1605, the buildings were searched twice. On the first occasion, yeomen of the guard ("beefeaters") discovered Fawkes with his woodpile. A further search was made by the suspicious guards at eleven at night. They found the gunpowder and arrested Fawkes, the only plotter present.

Catesby and three others died resisting arrest; the others, including Fawkes, were tried on January 27 1606, and executed. Parliament named November 5 as a day for national thanksgiving. Since the 19th century, the celebrations have taken a more rowdy form, with fireworks and the burning on bonfires of effigies of Fawkes called "guys".

The Pilgrim Fathers
c.1620

The Pilgrim Fathers crossed the Atlantic in the tiny Mayflower *and in 1620 founded the first lasting settlement in North America.*

The Pilgrims originally came from the north of England. They were serious, earnest people of Puritan disposition, known as Separatists because they wanted to form a separate church apart from the Church of England. This was against the law, and eventually they fled from the threat of imprisonment, to settle in the Netherlands.

They settled in Leyden in 1608 under the leadership of minister John Robinson. Life was hard, for they were farmers not used to city life, and were afraid of their children being tempted from their faith. They resolved to settle in the New World away from temptations of big cities. In 1620 they set sail in the *Speedwell*. At Southampton, they were joined by more Separatists in the *Mayflower*. They received a charter to settle in Virginia. The ships had not gone far when *Speedwell* sprang a leak, and they were forced to turn back. Finally, on September 6 1620, *Mayflower* left Plymouth, England on its own, with 120 Pilgrims.

The delays meant *Mayflower* was sailing when the Atlantic was roughest. It took 63 stormy days to cross the Atlantic. Most of the Pilgrims were seasick in their small and stifling cabins. On November 11 they anchored off the bleak Cape Cod. They decided to settle in Massachusetts not Virginia, and chose Plymouth across the bay. The first landing was made on December 11, on Plymouth Rock.

The settlers made the Mayflower Compact, to guarantee that government would be according to the wishes of the settlers, and affirmed their loyalty to King James. John Carver was elected Governor. The land was heavily wooded and inhospitable. Cabins were made of felled trees to provide shelter for the winter, which was already well advanced.

The work was exhausting, and there was little food, once *Mayflower* left, apart from fish. At one time disease reduced those active to six. The winter was fairly mild, but 44 were dead by April 1621, including Governor Carver. William Bradford replaced him, but the colony's survival owed much to Miles Standish, whose military skill kept those natives who were hostile at bay. They were helped by friendly Indians, who taught them how to catch fish and plant Indian corn. In November 1621 they celebrated a thanksgiving for the arrival of the *Fortune*, with food to supplement the harvest and the wild turkeys they caught in the woods. This festival is still celebrated in the United States, into which the original colony has grown.

The Pilgrims leave the Netherlands.

(Inset) The landing at Plymouth Rock.

THE ENGLISH REVOLUTION

Charles I
1600–49

Charles I was King of England and Scotland from 1625 to 1649. He was an unpopular monarch and attempted to raise revenue without consent, and to rule without Parliament. These moves brought on the English Civil War (1642–46, 1648). He was defeated at Marston Moor, 1644 and Naseby, 1645. In 1649 he was tried and executed by Parliament.

Charles was the second Stuart king, and he never lost either his Scots accent or a stammer. He was a shy, delicate but devious man. These characteristics, combined with a large conception of the power and rights of a king, caused Parliament to increasingly distrust him.

Charles's policies were unpopular from the start. He fought wars with France and Spain, which were costly and fruitless, and produced resentment. Parliament responded with the Petition of Right in 1628, a guarantee of freedom from arbitrary imprisonment, and the forced billetting of soldiers in citizens' homes. Charles accepted this because he needed money from Parliament, but it decided him to rule without Parliament, which he did for 11 years, getting money by customs dues and forced loans. He supported his Archbishop of Canterbury, Laud, in moving the Church towards Catholicism.

Laud's reforms provoked rebellion in Scotland in 1639. Defeats and the cost of the Army forced Charles to recall Parliament. Led by John Pym, the Short (April–May 1640) and Long Parliaments (Nov. 1640–1653) abolished many of the instruments of royal tyranny. The King allowed Laud and the Earl of Strafford, his chief advisor, to be punished by Parliament, but he refused to surrender control over Church or Army, which he believed was an essential right of the Crown. The House of Commons feared he would reverse his concessions if some form of permanent control was not found. Charles attempted to arrest five Members of Parliament, but, when he arrived with soldiers, they had fled; as he

(Left) The trial of Charles I.

(Below) The execution of Charles I.

said, "the birds had flown". The country moved towards war between Parliament and the King, who held his court in Oxford.

At first, the two sides were evenly matched, and the first battle, at Edgehill, was indecisive. Charles's followers were known as the Cavaliers, because of their colourful dress. Charles's most dashing commander was his nephew, Prince Rupert, who rode into battle followed by his little white dog. The tide turned once the Parliamentary Army was reorganized under Oliver Cromwell in 1645 (see opposite). Oxford was captured in 1646; the King escaped in disguise, and surrendered to the Scots, who were allies of Parliament. He hoped he could do a deal with them, but they handed him to Parliament when their forces left England in 1647. Parliament tried to make him rule as a constitutional monarch, subject to the commands of Parliament.

Charles made many promises, but at the same time plotted to regain the power he had lost. He attempted to do so with the aid of the Scots, but they were defeated by Cromwell at Preston in 1648. This time, the Army leaders decided to rid themselves of the King. He was tried by a tribunal of the House of Commons, made up only of those approved by the Army. Charles refused to recognize the legality of the tribunal, or that he could be tried by his subjects, and conducted himself with a quiet dignity. He won popular sympathy, but this could not prevent his execution by beheading outside the Banqueting Hall in Whitehall on January 30 1649.

Cavalier soldiers.

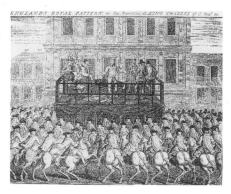

Oliver Cromwell

1599–1658

Oliver Cromwell was second-in-command of the Parliamentary Army in the Civil War. As leader of the Army, he was the virtual ruler of England from 1649 until his death. He subdued Scotland (battles of Dunbar 1650 and Worcester 1651) and Ireland (Drogheda 1649). In 1653 he was made Lord Protector. He built up the Navy, under Admiral Blake, and increased English territory in the West Indies.

Cromwell was a descendant of Henry VIII's advisor, Thomas Cromwell. He became a Member of Parliament, where he sided with those who opposed the King's arbitrary government. He was a devout Puritan, but for that time was unusually tolerant of other Christian sects, apart from Catholics.

When the King defied the Long Parliament, Cromwell returned home and raised a regiment of cavalry. These became known as the Ironsides. Cromwell was second-in-command of the Eastern Association armies of Parliament, and his cavalry played a crucial part in defeating Charles's Cavalier Army at Marston Moor in 1644.

In 1645, the New Model Army, a national army, was created to replace the regional groupings, and Cromwell became second-in-command. His soldiers were well-trained, disciplined and armed, and the Roundheads, as they were known, were now more than a match for the royal forces.

In 1648, the Army pressured Parliament into trying the King, and guaranteed the result of the trial by "Pride's Purge", in which a Colonel Pride excluded unsympathetic MPs. Cromwell was in the north at the time, having just defeated the Scots at Preston. He delayed agreeing to the trial of the King until he was convinced it was God's will. Such indecision was typical, though when his mind was made up, he always acted quickly and forcefully.

The King was found guilty of treason,

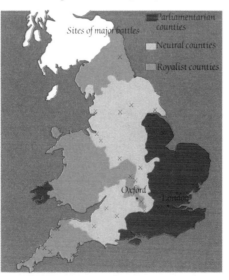

(Left) The battles of the English Civil War. Parliament dominated the South and East, Charles the North and West.

On April 20 1653, Cromwell used musketeers to dissolve the unruly Rump Parliament, leaving himself in sole control.

and executed in 1649. A republican "Commonwealth" was proclaimed, ruled by a Council of State. There were many diverse elements in Parliament and the Army, some of whom wanted revolutionary social change ("Levellers"), and others who did not. Cromwell kept a balance between them, resisting revolution. He insisted on religious toleration, when the "Rump" Parliament (the remnant of the Long Parliament) wanted persecution of dissent.

Cromwell dissolved the unrepresentative Parliament and was made Lord Protector, and virtual dictator. Cromwell himself searched for a new and more representative form of government, without success. He refused the Army's offer of the crown. He disagreed with radical puritan measures that Parliament had pushed through, such as the abolition of Christmas. Although a Puritan, Cromwell was by no means a killjoy; he was criticised for allowing mixed dancing at his daughter's wedding.

Cromwell defeated and then made peace with the Dutch, retaining New Amsterdam (now New York), which had been captured. Much of Oliver Cromwell's work was removed by the restoration of the monarch in 1660, but he remains as one of the greatest Englishmen, a fighter against tyranny and a pioneer of toleration of minority religious sects.

(Left) The battles of the English Civil War. Parliament dominated the South and East, Charles the North and West. (Far left) Cromwell's "Ironsides". Armour was in fact little use against the new guns at close range.

Charles II
1630–85

Charles II was King of Britain from 1660 to 1685. His reign saw a reaction to Puritan severity in art, fashion and the King's own behaviour. In 1665 many died in the Great Plague, and in 1666 London was devastated by the Great Fire.

Charles was the eldest son of Charles I, and from the age of 12 was involved in the turmoil of the Civil War (see pages 52–53). He developed a cynicism and realistic judgement of men in the hard conditions he experienced as a youth. In 1645 he went into exile, in Jersey, France and the Netherlands. After the execution of his father in 1649, he landed in Scotland to head a rising against Parliament. The Scots were defeated by Cromwell at Dunbar (September 3 1650). Charles persevered, and his Scottish army invaded England in 1651, only to be decisively defeated by Cromwell at Worcester exactly a year after Dunbar. Charles hid after the battle in an oak tree at Boscobel, and after six weeks there and in other hiding places, once

A fire in a baker's shop spread to destroy most of London (1666).

The Restoration; Charles leaves exile in the Netherlands to claim his throne.

During the wars, Dutch ships often raided up the Thames and Medway.

more fled abroad.

Charles spent the next nine years a poor refugee in France and the Netherlands. After Cromwell's death, Charles's minister, the Duke of Clarendon negotiated his return with General Monck, the most powerful of the Parliamentarian generals. Charles made a declaration that he would allow more religious freedom than his father, and give an amnesty to combatants in the Civil War, and on 25 May 1660, Charles landed at Dover, to popular acclaim.

Charles' main aim as king was to ensure he need "never go on his travels again". He avoided political controversy. Such matters did not in fact interest him very much, for he was a lazy and pleasure-loving man. He was known as the "merry monarch". The country as a whole enjoyed the relaxation of Puritan restraints. The theatre began again, and flourished under the patronage of the King. The Restoration period is characterized by this new freedom; by wit, jollity, and a moral laxity in which the King gave the lead. Charles was tall and athletic, and acquired many mistresses, including Nell Gwynn the orange-girl. He had 14 illegitimate children, but no legitimate offspring.

Charles gave a pardon to all those who had fought in the Civil War, except

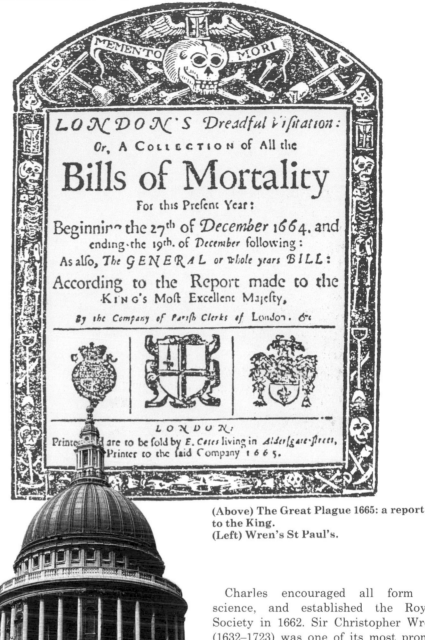

(Above) The Great Plague 1665: a report to the King.
(Left) Wren's St Paul's.

those who had sentenced his father to death, 11 of whom were executed. Charles made an alliance with Louis XIV in order to try to destroy the Dutch, who were England's trade rivals. He hoped by this to make the Crown financially independent from Parliament. He found MPs were now very independent-minded as a result of power they had won in the Civil War, and this made absolute royal rule impossible.

The biggest crisis of the reign was over Catholicism, in 1779–81, when a false rumour of a plot by Catholics to kill Charles was circulated by Titus Oates, a renegade priest. The Exclusion Crisis followed; an attempt to have Charles' Catholic brother James banned from succeeding to the throne. A subsidy from Louis did enable Charles to rule without Parliament for his last four years. A secret condition for this was that he convert to Catholicism; aware this would be unpopular, he only did so on his deathbed.

England was unsuccessful in fighting the Dutch, who won sweeping victories, even raiding up the Thames. However, in the peace settlement, Britain retained control of New Holland (New York colony), which had been won by Cromwell.

Charles employed Samuel Pepys (1633–1703) to help rebuild the Navy so that it could meet the Dutch challenge, and Pepys fought against corruption in the Navy Board. Pepys' greatest claim to fame, however, was his diary, kept from 1660 to 1669. It is an invaluable record of gossip, court scandal, the Plague, the Fire of London, and the Dutch sailing up the Thames. It was kept in secret code, which was not decyphered until the 19th century.

Charles encouraged all form of science, and established the Royal Society in 1662. Sir Christopher Wren (1632–1723) was one of its most prominent members. A skilled mathematician and astronomer, he turned to architecture in 1663, and in 1666 was already working on a restoration plan for St Paul's Cathedral, when it was destroyed in the Great Fire, along with two-thirds of the city. His grand design for the whole city was rejected as too expensive, but he built 53 churches in London, including his masterpiece, the new St Paul's, completed in 1711. He was strongly influenced by buildings such as St Peter's he had seen in Rome. Other famous buildings of his include the Royal Hospital Chelsea, Greenwich Hospital and parts of Hampton Court palace.

Louis XIV
1638–1715

Louis XIV was King of France for 72 years (1643–1715), the longest reign in European history. He fought a succession of major wars. He created a magnificent court at Versailles, and French culture dominated Europe.

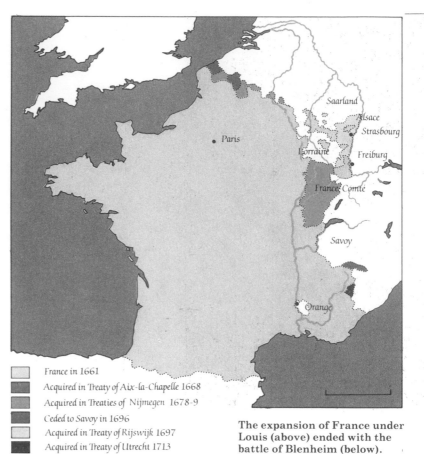

☐	France in 1661
▨	Acquired in Treaty of Aix-la-Chapelle 1668
▨	Acquired in Treaties of Nijmegen 1678-9
▨	Ceded to Savoy in 1696
☐	Acquired in Treaty of Rijswijk 1697
■	Acquired in Treaty of Utrecht 1713

The expansion of France under Louis (above) ended with the battle of Blenheim (below).

Louis became king at the age of five. In his boyhood, while Cardinal Mazarin ruled as regent in his stead, France suffered a number of revolts, called *frondes*. Louis had to flee Paris on three occasions, and once had to pretend to be asleep whilst the rebels passed through his bedroom. These experiences gave the boy Louis a determination to be a strong ruler.

Louis came of age in 1651, but did not begin to take part in government until the death of Mazarin in 1661. He took his job as king very seriously, working on government matters for eight or so hours each day. As well as being a working ruler, he was the centre of a brilliant court and a notorious womanizer. He had a succession of mistresses, and some 11 illegitimate children. He married one of his mistresses, Madame de Maintenon, in secret in 1683 or 1684.

Louis built upon the work of Mazarin and the great advisor of the previous reign, Cardinal Richelieu, who had moved the French monarchy towards absolute control of the government of the country. He ruled France personally, through trusted ministers, notably Jean-Baptiste Colbert, and professional administrators. Neither the *Parlement* (parliament) nor the nobles were given any part in government. Louis declared accurately, "L'etat c'est moi" (I am the state).

Louis increased the splendour and majesty of the monarchy, which became the envy of and the example for all budding absolute monarchs in Europe. Under his patronage, French art, literature and architecture entered a golden age. Great playwrights such as Molière and Racine put on plays at the Court. Louis built the great palace at Versailles outside Paris, one of the wonders of the civilized world. At the centre of it all was the magnificent and handsome figure of Louis, who became known as the "Sun King". Absolutism even extended to culture, however, and it was only styles approved by the King that were allowed to flourish.

The same applied in politics and religion; liberal or progressive ideas such as those of René Descartes, philosopher and mathematician, were banned. As he grew older, and especially as he came under the influence of Madame de Maintenon, Louis became more intoler-ant towards religious dissenters, and the French Protestants, the Huguenots, were persecuted. Many had to leave France, and go to the Netherlands, England or America. In foreign affairs, Louis followed an ambitious and aggressive policy. He involved France in many wars, most of which he started, for two motives; to defend France, and to add to the territories he ruled over. He pushed French borders to the river Rhine, and into modern-day Belgium. He succeeded in installing his grandson Philip as King of Spain. Overseas, France colonized Canada, Louisiana and parts of India.

Louis' chief enemies were the Holy Roman Emperor, Leopold of Austria, Spain (which ruled Belgium) and the Protestant United Provinces of the Netherlands. He was able to buy the alliance of Charles II of England, and England fought wars against the Dutch on the French side. He also formed an alliance against Leopold with the Muslim Turks, who were threatening Vienna, the Austrian capital. This attracted much hostility in Christian Europe, and together with Louis' great power and ambition it provoked other nations to combine against him. The wars of his last years against this combination, though they succeeded in making Philip King of Spain, were disastrously expensive, and culminated in defeats at the hands of the Austrian

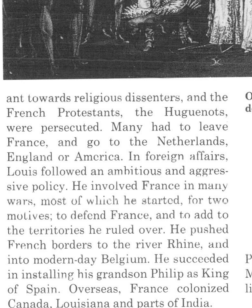

One of Louis XIV's many lovers, Madame de la Vallière, with the King.

Prince Eugen and the English Duke of Marlborough at Blenheim (1704), Ramillies (1706) and Malplaquet (1709).

Alongside all the magnificence there were many problems. Louis cared much for the prestige of himself and France, but little for the condition of the French people. The succession of wars was immensely costly, and the monarchy that Louis handed to his successor was magnificent but bankrupt. The heaviest burden of taxation lay on the middle-classes and the peasants; those least able to pay. The rich nobles were exempt from taxes, but played little part in government, and had been reduced to nothing more than dandified courtiers. This situation was to explode in the French Revolution some 75 years after Louis' death.

Louis outlived both his son and his grandson, and his successor was his great-grandson, Louis XV, who was only five years old.

Sir Isaac Newton
1642–1727

Sir Isaac Newton was a brilliant English scientist, and the father of modern science. He was the first to show that nature follows constant laws. His theory of gravitation explained the motion of the planets and stars.

Newton was the son of a gentleman farmer who died before his son was born. He was a tiny baby and not expected to survive. Newton lived to be 84! Isaac's mother left him to be brought up by his grandmother for nine years, contributing to a sense of insecurity shown in his later life in a violent temper against anyone who suggested his discoveries were mistaken or were not completely his own work.

Newton proved unsuitable for his first job as a manager of a farm, preferring to spend his time thinking under a tree. He became intrigued by the forces of nature, and asked himself whether the force that made an apple fall off a tree to the ground was the same as that which kept the moon circling the Earth.

Newton went to Cambridge University, and by the time he had graduated in 1665, he had made important mathematical discoveries. He became Professor of Mathematics at Cambridge. He began research into light, and established that colour comes not from an object, but is in the light itself.

Newton's greatest work was made public in 1687, though he had formulated it some years before. His book, *Mathematical Principles of Natural Philosophy* was so advanced that it was said there were not a dozen men in Europe who could understand it. His three laws laid down the crucial principle of gravitation; that every particle in the universe attracts every other with a force in proportion to its mass. This provided the answer to his question under the apple tree. 'What goes up must come down' was a universal principle, applying as well to planets as to apples. The idea that nature could be reduced to such laws was the beginning of modern scientific method.

Newton's personal life was punctuated by controversies with fellow scientists, stemming from Newton's inability to take criticism without exploding into a rage. He had two nervous breakdowns, one produced by the death of his mother, and the other by a quarrel with his close friend, Fatio du

Duillier, a Swiss scholar.

Newton sponsored a large group of young scientists from earnings as warden of the Royal Mint. He was the first scientist to be knighted, in 1705, and was a domineering President of the Royal Society, though towards the end of his life he frequently dozed off at meetings. He was buried in Westminster Abbey, as befitted one of his greatness.

(Left) Among Newton's important inventions was the reflecting telescope: shown here in the old observing room, Greenwich.
(Top right) The Newtonian ordered universe, depicted by poet **William Blake (1757–1827).**
(Below) Newton's solution to the problem of curves of descent, in his own handwriting.

John Wesley

1703–91

John Wesley was an English religious leader who founded the Christian Methodist movement.

John Wesley was the son of a Church of England rector. When he was six the rectory was burned down, and John was only just rescued. John and his brother Charles went to Oxford University in the 1720s, and founded a religious study group, known as the Holy Club. Their emphasis on methodical study and devotion earned its members the nickname of "methodists". Under the leadership of John, who was ordained priest in the Church of England in 1728, they would fast for two days a week, and visit prisons and workhouses to take clothes, medicine and books to the inmates.

In 1735, John went out to Georgia in America, to look after the spiritual lives of the colonists. On the stormy journey, he was impressed by the spiritual serenity of some Christians from Moravia (in modern Czechoslovakia). His mission was not a success, for the colonists were hostile to his strict attitude, particularly when he refused communion to a woman who had married another man in preference to him. Before leaving in December 1737, he did however set up some methodist societies.

Back in London, he renewed contacts with the Lutheran Moravians, and it was at one of their meetings, during a reading of Luther, that Wesley received a spiritual awakening. He became determined to preach the message of salvation by faith. His enthusiasm aroused hostility in the staid Church of England of the time, and under the prompting of the preacher George Whitfield, he set out to preach to the masses who belonged to no church. He started at Bristol in April 1739, where he preached in the open air to 3,000 people.

Wesley soon attracted a following, which he organized into methodist societies. Most churchmen saw this as rabble-rousing, so Wesley used laymen as his preachers and administrators. He preferred to remain in the Church of England, but in 1784, when bishops refused to ordain his preachers, he ordained them himself. His brother, also an active preacher, remained in the Church of England, and contributed many famous hymns to it. They had earlier quarrelled when Charles prevented John marrying his housekeeper.

Wesley travelled some 250,000 miles (400,000 km), giving 50,000 sermons. He was the foremost figure in the 18th century religious revival, and brought Christianity to many in the new industrial cities.

(Above right) The first Methodist Conference, 1744.
(Right) Laying the cornerstone of the first Methodist chapel, Bristol, 1739.

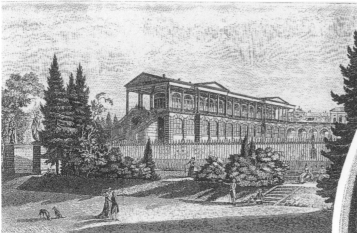

The Palace of Czarskoe Selo at the time of Catherine the Great.

Catherine the Great
1729–1796

Catherine II was Empress of Russia from 1762 to 1796. She continued the policy of Czar Peter the Great with the centralization of government, the introduction of Western European culture and the expansion of Russian territory.

Catherine was not a Russian; she was born in Stettin, Germany and originally called Princess Sophie Augusta Fredericka. She was brought to Russia by Empress Elizabeth to marry the heir to the throne. She was received into the Russian Orthodox Church in 1744, as one of the conditions of the marriage, and took the Russian name Catherine Alexeyevna. She married the future Peter III in 1745.

Catherine regarded her husband as unfit to rule, and shortly after he became Czar (Emperor) in 1762, she overthrew him with help from her lover Gregory Orlov and the palace guards. Soon after, Peter was murdered.

Catherine was very capable politically, and followed the trend of the time of strong personal rule by the monarch, amounting to dictatorship (absolutism). Although advancing a number of men, usually her lovers, to positions of authority, she always remained her own boss, and was personally responsible both for the modernizations carried out

in Russia in her reign, and for the great cruelty that was practised.

Catherine's policies were a strange mixture of two different philosophies. She was an open admirer of the Western European Enlightenment. This was a movement that grew up in the 17th century, around the new scientific theories of men like Newton, and the philosophies of the Frenchman, René Descartes and the English John Locke. These were based on reason rather than religion or tradition, and the idea that human behaviour followed laws and patterns as Newton has demonstrated nature did. Such ideas were behind the growth of the modern state in the 18th century, with a professional civil service and regular legal codes. It was also the basis of absolutism, which aimed to strengthen central authority over independent groups like church and nobles.

Catherine extended royal control over all the area of Russia she ruled, rather than just the two capitals, St Petersburg and Moscow as previously. She moder-

nized and liberalized the economy, and plundered Church lands. Priests became little more than another form of civil servant. She introduced social reforms along lines suggested by enlightened Western thinkers, and her reign saw a great influx into Russia of Western culture; Italian opera, painting and sculpture, and French philosophy and manners. She made permanent Peter the Great's introduction of French as the official language of the court.

At the same time, however, she adhered to the ways of her predecessors. The great mass of the Russian people were poor peasants who unlike their counterparts in France and England, were still serfs; that is, they were the property of their lords, who could do with them as they wanted. Catherine did nothing to relieve their plight, indeed she greatly added to their number by spreading serfdom to areas she conquered, and applying it to those who worked what had been Church land.

Despite her attempts to concentrate

(Left) Gregory Potemkin, talented commander of Catherine's armies. He was one of Catherine's many favourites to reach high office.
(Right) The rebel Emelian Pugachev, a Don Cossack. He claimed to be Czar Peter III, and attracted 20–30,000 followers with promises of restoring the old religion, land and freedom. After capture in September 1774, he was taken to Moscow in an iron cage and brutally executed.
(Bottom) Street life in Catherine the Great's Russia.

all authority in the hands of the Crown and the state organization controlled by the Crown, Catherine in fact gave increased independence to the nobility. All the top jobs in the Civil Service were reserved for nobles, and this was a great barrier to any attempts to lessen their power. It was the lower classes who suffered; lords could sentence serfs to hard labour, and complaints by serfs against their lords were forbidden on pain of whipping with the *knout* (a vicious whip) and life imprisonment.

The result was much discontent amongst the classes whose hopes had been raised by Catherine's apparent liberalism, and the conquered peoples such as Poles and Cossacks she brought under the Russian system. The worst outbreak was the Pugachev rebellion of 1773–74 which was put down with extreme cruelty and much bloodshed. The leader, a Cossack called Pugachev, was taken to Moscow in an iron cage, and his body broken on the wheel by whipping. He was then beheaded, dismembered and burnt.

In foreign affairs, Catherine conquered lands from Turkey on the Black Sea coast, including the Crimea, and participated in three successive partitions of Poland after which that country ceased to exist. Russia was enlarged by 200,000 square miles (517,000 square kilometres), and 7 million people, and was poised for the extension of power into Asia in the 19th century that made Russia the huge country it is today. Her generals, Suvorov and Potemkin (one of her lovers) won Europe-wide renown in the campaigns against Turkey, and against the French Revolution, to which Catherine was as much opposed as she was to liberalism at home. The greatest Russian liberal thinker of her time, Radischev, was exiled to Siberia.

Catherine was personally a charming, warm person, whilst at the same time ruthless, harsh and unscrupulous, possessing a great deal of political cunning allied with great intelligence. She was a woman of inexhaustible passion: at least 21 of her lovers are known by name, and there were countless others. Her military victories and the brilliance of her court earned her the title "the Great" in her own lifetime. When she took possession of the Black Sea provinces, her fleet was decorated as that of Cleopatra, Queen of Egypt, and she was attended by many of the monarchs of Europe. Russia had arrived as a European power.

Robert Clive
1725–74

Robert Clive was a soldier and administrator, and the man most responsible for India coming under British rule. He defeated the French and their Indian allies at Arcot (1751), Calcutta (1757) and Plassey (1757), all with inferior numbers. He was Governor of Bengal 1757–60, and again in 1764–67.

Clive was the son of an English Member of Parliament and was an extremely unruly and moody child. At 18, he went to Madras in India, as a clerk in the British East India Company. Weighed down by boredom and loneliness Clive tried twice to shoot himself. On both occasions the pistol failed to fire.

His opportunity came, however, with war, and in 1751 he demonstrated his talent as a tactician by capturing the fort of Arcot with 200 Europeans and 300 Sepoys (Indian troops) and defending it for 53 days against 10,000 Indian and French soldiers.

Clive returned to England in 1753 and was awarded a diamond-hilted sword for his services. He returned to India in 1755 as a lieutenant-colonel. British trade centred on Calcutta, the wealthiest city in India and the envy of neighbouring rulers. In 1756, Prince Siraj-ud-Dowlah, Nawab of Bengal, captured Calcutta and locked his 146 British captives in a small room that became notorious as the "Black Hole of Calcutta". 123 died of suffocation before morning. After recapturing the city, Clive decisively defeated the Nawab at Plassey in 1757, with 3,200 men against 68,000 soldiers and 50 elephants. Clive followed this up by engineering the deposition of Siraj, leaving the British as rulers of Bengal, and in a dominant position in the rest of India. Clive received great rewards from the new Nawab, Mir Jaffir, and returned to England a rich man, with large Indian estates.

Clive was made Baron Clive of Plassey, served as an MP, and was knighted in 1764. He served in India again in 1764-67, and purged much corruption from the East India Company's affairs. This made him enemies and he had to defend his conduct in Parliament, and justify the money he received from Jaffir. Although cleared of all charges, Clive felt that he was depressed by the episode. He felt that he was treated like a "mere sheep-stealer". Suffering ill-health, a dependence on opium and increasing fits of depression, in 1774 he finally took his own life by cutting his throat.

Clive and his ally, Mir Jaffir, the new Nawab of Bengal, after Plassey, 1757.

Captain Cook
1728–79

James Cook was an intrepid English explorer. He was a man of many skills who made great contributions to European knowledge of the lands of the Pacific Ocean. On three voyages, 1768–71, 1772–75 and 1776, he surveyed and explored New Zealand, Eastern Australia, Hawaii and many other Pacific islands.

James Cook was born and raised in a small coastal town in the north of England. He became a shopkeeper's apprentice, but was more interested in the sea, and joined the Royal Navy in 1755. 1759 found him master of HMS *Mercury,* fighting the French on the St Lawrence River in Canada. He was already becoming renowned as a navigator and map-maker, and this skill brought him to the attention of the Royal Society. He was commissioned to lead an expedition to the southern hemisphere to observe the transit of planet Venus – the movement of the planet Venus across the face of the sun.

Cook was the ideal man to head expeditions into unknown and possibly dangerous waters. As well as being a skilled navigator, he kept meticulous records, essential for scientific purposes, and was to show some medical skill. He sailed from Plymouth on August 26 1768 on board the *Endeavour,* a small ship of 370 tons, carrying 84 officers and crew. They entered the Pacific round Cape Horn, and first stopped at Tahiti, which Cook named King George III Island. The natives rowed to meet them and gave them branches as symbols of peace. Cook stayed three months, studying the Tahitians and their ways of life.

Three months after leaving Tahiti, New Zealand was sighted. Cook surveyed the coast of this new land, which he claimed for Britain, and then sailed through Cook Strait between the two islands. He then explored the east coast of Australia, which he called New South Wales. Others had only seen the west and north and found it a barren land, but Cook found New South Wales green and fertile and suitable for colonization.

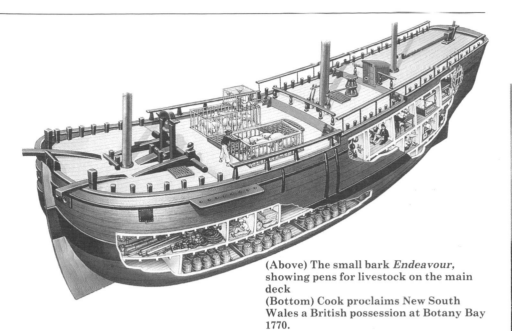

(Above) The small bark *Endeavour,* showing pens for livestock on the main deck
(Bottom) Cook proclaims New South Wales a British possession at Botany Bay 1770.

On his second voyage, Cook sailed further south than any man before him, and established that there was not another continent close to the south of Australia. Once again many islands were discovered and mapped. In 1776, at the age of 48, he set out again. He landed in Hawaii, which had been discovered before, but forgotten, and named the archipelago the Sandwich Islands, after the Earl of Sandwich, the First Lord of the Admiralty.

Cook sailed north in search of a north-west passage to the Atlantic round the north of Canada, but was stopped north of the Bering Strait by ice. He returned to Hawaii, and met his death. Cook had always been kind towards natives, so it was not fitting he should meet the end he did. He stepped ashore to resolve a dispute between some of his sailors and natives over a stolen ship's boat, but could not prevent a scuffle, during which he was killed.

James Wolfe

1727–59

James Wolfe was a British soldier, whose decisive victory at Quebec in 1759 resulted in Canada becoming part of the British Empire. Wolfe died in the battle.

At the start of the 1750s, eastern Canada was part of a French empire that stretched down the Mississippi River to New Orleans. The French were often involved in skirmishes with the British as the latter extended their colonies inland from the coast. In 1756, the Seven Years War broke out in Europe between Britain and France, and fighting took place around the world, mostly in North America, where it was known as the French-Indian War. Wolfe was sent out to fight in this war in 1758.

James Wolfe was a frail and studious young man, by no means a typical military hero. However, he had plenty of energy and determination, and a gift for origi-nality that was to win him lasting fame. He entered the army at the age of 14.

In 1758, when he was only 31, Wolfe was sent to North America as a Briga-dier-General. He played an important part in the capture of a French fort at Louisburg, and William Pitt, the Prime Minister, appointed him Major-General with the task of capturing Quebec.

The subsequent operation has become an epic of military history. After three months siege, the British had made no impression on the impregnable position of the French. Wolfe became depressed by the failure of all his attacks and was enfeebled by disease. He turned to a bold solution. During the night of September 12 and 13, he crossed the St Lawrence River above the town, and surprised the French sentries at the cove now named after him. He and his men then climbed the supposedly unscalable cliffs, in the dark.

When day broke, Wolfe had about 4,000 men drawn up for battle on the Plains of Abraham to the southwest of Quebec, and had taken the French completely by surprise. The French were soundly defeated. Wolfe was wounded three times, and died before the pursuit of the French ended. He knew he had won, and said, "I die contented".

The war was ended with the Treaty of Paris in 1763, in which the British gained possession of Canada and all the French lands east of the Mississippi.

(Below) The capture of Quebec.

(Left) The death of Wolfe. The French commander, Montcalm, was also killed.

George III
1738–1820

George III was King of Britain 1760–1820. Canada, New Zealand, Australia, and India were added to the British Empire, though the 13 colonies of North America gained independence as the United States. Britain was at war with France in the Seven Years War (1756–63), and the Napoleonic Wars (1796–1815).

George's predecessors, George I and George II were born in Germany, spoke little English and cared more for their lands in Hanover than Britain. Their reigns had seen the office of prime minister become established as that of head of government, in the hands of Robert Walpole and William Pitt. George III was, in contrast, an Englishman to the core. He attempted to restore the pre-eminent role of the king in government, with disastrous results. George removed Pitt, the great minister of George II's reign, and placed power in the hands of his own men.

George III is best remembered as the king who drove the American colonies into revolt. George was no bloodthirsty tyrant, but his ill-advised attempts at strong royal government provoked great resentment in America. Increased taxes and customs duties were imposed by the government of Lord North; the result was the "Boston Tea Party", when colonists disguised as Indians tipped a cargo of tea into Boston harbour in protest against tea duties. Eventually the colonists turned to open revolt.

During George's long reign, the monarchy's prestige fell sharply, largely as a result of his interference in government. It was not helped by occasional fits, caused by a hereditary physical disease, porphyra, though this was officially diagnosed as madness. In 1811,

the king suffered a more permanent fit, together with blindness, and his dissolute son, the future George IV, ruled in his stead as Prince Regent.

Although his reign was far from successful, George's personal life was beyond reproach. In many ways he was better fitted to be a country squire than a king. His favourite hobby was agriculture, and he set up a farm at Windsor, earning himself the name "Farmer George". He lived in faithful domesticity with his Queen, and had nine sons and six daughters.

On the credit side, George should be compared to contemporaries such as Louis XV of France or Joseph II of Austria, who ruled as absolute monarchs. It would have needed a strong king to do this, and George was of very average ability. He never tried to do away with Parliament, and did eventually allow capable ministers like Pitt the Younger (prime minister at the age of 24) to come forward. The movement to constitutional monarchy of the early 18th century was not permanently halted.

(Top right) An Indian prince receiving an East India Company representative. British troops soon followed.
(Right) Events such as the Boston Massacre (1770) provoked the American colonies into revolt.

Franklin was the fifteenth of seventeen children of a tallow chandler (candle maker) in Boston, Massachusetts. He was largely self-educated. He was apprenticed to his half-brother as a printer, but chafed at the restrictions placed on apprentices learning a trade, and ran away to Philadelphia. There he quickly moved from printing into journalism. His *Poor Richard's Almanac*, published yearly between 1732 and 1757 was one of the most popular books of the colonial period in America. Many of the sayings contained in it, some of them borrowed, some composed by Franklin, have become American proverbs.

Franklin had a creative and original mind. He was quickly drawn into public service; he created the first fire service in Pennsylvania in 1736, became postmaster in 1737, and founded the American Philosophical Society in 1743. In 1752, he earned international recognition with his experiments with electricity. He flew a kite in a thunderstorm, and a spark jumped from a key he had tied to the kite's string to the ground. From this experiment, which showed

Benjamin Franklin
1706–90

Benjamin Franklin was an American statesman, administrator and scientist. He played a leading role in the American Revolution, being involved in the Declaration of Independence, and the drafting of the United States Constitution. He made important discoveries concerning the nature of electricity.

Franklin's first machine for generating electricity.

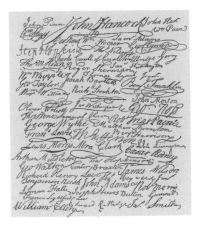

The signatures on the Declaration of Independence.

George Washington
1732–1799

George Washington commanded the American forces during the War of Independence, 1776–83. He won the final victory at Yorktown. He chaired the Constitutional Convention, and was the first President of the United States, 1789–97.

George Washington was a wealthy plantation owner in Virginia, who at the age of 20 inherited the extensive estate of Mount Vernon, including up to 50 slaves. He acquired a taste for soldiering while serving on the British side in the war of 1754–63 against France. He showed his bravery at the battle at Fort Duquesne in 1755 when two horses were shot from under him, and his clothes were cut by four bullets, while fighting by the side of his commander, who was killed. He rose to the rank of colonel, and was given command of all the Virginian troops.

Washington's request for a permanent commission in the army was refused by the British, and he retired from soldiering. He then lived a lavish aristocratic life at Mount Vernon, until 1775, when he was called upon to take command of the colonists who were in revolt against the British.

lightning was electric, he devised the first lightning conductor. It was a dangerous experiment; two others who tried it were killed.

Franklin became increasingly involved in politics. He was sent to England as the colonial representative, from 1757 to 1762, and again from 1764 to 1775. In England he was much sought after in social circles, and admitted into the Royal Society for his scientific attainments. He managed to change some of George III's policies, but these changes did not stop the high taxation of the colonists, which had brought them to the brink of revolt.

Franklin returned home, and took his stand with those seeking independence. He was one of the few internationally known Americans, and his stand influenced many others. He helped Thomas Jefferson to draw up the Declaration of Independence of July 4, 1776, and signed that historic document. He then made a vital mission to France, which secured French armed support for the American cause. When the war ended with the surrender of the British at Yorktown in 1783, it was Franklin who negotiated the Treaty of Paris, by which the British finally acknowledged the independence of the United States. Franklin was an important member of the Constitutional Convention of 1787 to 1788, which after much discussion drew up the United States Constitution.

Tensions between the colonists and the British Government had been building up for some time. The British maintained that Parliament had a right to make laws covering the colonies, including the levying of taxes, even though the Americans were not represented, culminating on a tax on tea, and the Boston Tea Party in 1773 (when colonists threw tea into the harbour). Shots were exchanged at Lexington and Concord in 1775, and a revolutionary Continental Congress was called. Independence was declared on July 4, 1776.

The struggle lasted for seven years, during which time the Americans suffered many setbacks. Washington was not a brilliant tactician, and suffered a bad defeat at Brandywine Creek in 1777. However, his great strength was his ability to hold the confidence of his army. Throughout a long winter, he kept them together at Valley Forge, despite the fact that many of them were near starvation and barefoot. This was crucial, for in the following year the French entered the war on the American side. French assistance swung the balance, but it was Washington who struck the decisive blow in 1781 by surrounding the British at Yorktown and forcing their surrender. The British left their last base in New York in 1783, after peace was signed in Paris.

There were many differences between the individual states of the US, and Washington feared they might drift apart. He was a leading figure in calling the Constitutional Convention in 1787. As President of the Convention, he worked hard to ensure a constitution that preserved states rights, but within a secure union. He was such a respected figure that there was no other nomination to be first President. He served in this office for eight years, and as he had done during the war he played an important role in ensuring the United States survived as a single unified nation. He died in 1799, after catching pneumonia by riding during a blizzard, and his death was marked with respect not only in the United States, but also in Britain and France.

Thomas Paine
1737–1809

Thomas Paine was a political journalist, who contributed to the winning of US independence. His chief works were Common Sense, *the* Crisis Papers *and* Rights of Man.

Thomas Paine's strident declarations of the rights of the common man aroused extreme emotions of both agreement and hostility. They are depicted in this contemporary cartoon by Gillray.

Paine was born in Norfolk, England, and at the age of 13 went into his Quaker father's profession of corset-maker. His was a relentless spirit, and he moved through a rapid succession of jobs, and two marriages. In 1772 he met Benjamin Franklin in London, who advised him to go to America. In 1774, he arrived in Philadelphia, and became editor of the *Pennsylvania Magazine*. When the American Revolution broke out, Paine argued in his newspaper that Americans should demand complete independence. He repeated this in stronger terms in *Common Sense*, his most influential book, which sold over 500,000 copies within a few months. *Common Sense* played an influential part in rallying people behind the Declaration of Independence in 1776.

Paine's most significant contributions to the course of the fighting against the British, were the sixteen *Crisis Papers* (1776–83). The first one began, "these are the times that try men's souls". Washington circulated this stirring patriotic pamphlet amongst his troops at Valley Forge, and considered it played an important part in raising their low morale during the hard winter of 1776–77. At the end of the war, Washington supported the penniless Paine's plea for a pension from Congress. Paine had made no money on his books so they would sell cheaply and therefore reach a wider audience. Paine retired to a farm, and kept his restless mind occupied with inventions, among them a smokeless candle.

Paine had been in France in 1781, and had brought back important supplies of money, clothing and ammunition. When the French Revolution broke out in 1789, Paine was in England, and in *Rights of Man* (1791), vigorously defended the revolutionaries. The British Government banned the book, which also included a scheme for popular education, old age pensions and poor relief, and ordered him arrested as a threat to the established order. Fortunately, Paine had gone to Paris, where he had been elected a member of the revolutionary National Convention. In England he was declared an outlaw; in France he was imprisoned by Robespierre for opposing the Terror (see page 71). He was released on the fall of Robespierre in 1794, but did not return to the United States until 1802, where he found he was held in contempt for attacks on religion in *The Age of Reason*, which he had written in jail.

Paine died in poverty. Ten years later, his bones were taken to England by an admirer, but were lost in transit, and never received the worthy funeral that was intended.

Daniel Boone
1734 1820

Daniel Boone was an early American pioneer, influential in the exploration and colonization of Kentucky. He became a folk-hero as a result of his enterprise and exploits in fights with the Indians.

Boone's first view of Kentucky, 1767. He spent the next six years hunting and exploring the region, matching his wits against the Shawnee Indians.

By the second half of the 18th century, the eastern coast of what became the United States was fully settled by Europeans. Pioneering spirits began to push inland, through the Appalachian mountains. West of Virginia and North Carolina was land designated Indian territory, and beyond that were the French lands of Louisiana.

Daniel Boone was largely uneducated, and was a notoriously poor speller. He was a blacksmith and teamster (in charge of a team of horses) during the war with the French (1754–63), and escaped the defeat at Fort Duquesne, in which Washington distinguished himself, by fleeing on one of his horses. He subsequently began to take an interest in the unexplored frontier areas. In 1769 he penetrated through the Cumberland Gap in the Appalachian mountains into Kentucky, and spent two years as a trapper, always keeping one step ahead of the Shawnee Indians. In 1773 he decided to settle in Kentucky with his family. Due to Indian attacks, another five families who started with them turned back, but the Boones continued, and settled on the Church River.

Boone went on to lay out the Wilderness Road, founded Boonesborough on the Kentucky River, and was engaged by the Transylvania land settlement company to guide prospective settlers. In 1778, he was captured by some Shawnees. He cooperated with them for a while, and was adopted into the tribe with the name "Sheltowee" (Big Turtle).

During the War of Independence, Boone was captured by the British, feigned cooperation and escaped, rushing over 150 miles to alert Boonesborough, which was then able to resist the British attack. Boone was a lieutenant-colonel of militia in the war, and distinguished himself in a number of actions against the British and their Indian allies.

After the war, Boone had trouble establishing his right to lands he had settled, and ever restless, moved further west, to settle in what was then French territory, in Missouri. When this area became part of the United States in 1803, under the "Louisiana Purchase", he again had difficulty proving his right to land, for Boone was a man of the outdoors, with no head for paperwork. Eventually he was given a grant by Congress in recognition of his services during the war. He died in Missouri in 1820.

THE FRENCH REVOLUTION

Maximilien Robespierre
1758–94

Georges Danton
1759–94

Robespierre led the radical wing of the French Revolution, which began in 1789. He came to dominate the government, and started the Reign of Terror.
Danton was the Revolution's finest orator. Justice Minister, in 1792, he later chaired the Committee of Public Safety. Both were executed.

Maximilien Robespierre was a lawyer who made a name for himself defending the poor and attacking absolute royal power. In May 1789, he went as a representative to the Estates-General at Versailles. This was a French form of parliament. It had not met since 1614, as the French rulers were absolutists, dedicated to ruling personally. It was called in 1789 because the Government was desperately short of money and needed new taxes.

The delegates refused to approve any taxes without a relaxation of royal power, and reform of the tax system, which reinforced the divisions in society, and put most burden on the lower classes. The nobles wanted a limit to absolutism, which had reduced their own power, and the common people wanted greater equality. King Louis XVI refused any reduction of his

power, encouraged by his wife Marie Antoinette. He dismissed the Estates, and closed their chamber, but they gathered in the royal tennis court at Versailles and took the famous "Tennis Court Oath" not to disband. Led by the fiery Honoré Mirabeau, they renamed themselves the National Assembly and determined on making a new constitution.

In Paris, there was excitement at these events, and on July 14 1789 Parisians stormed the Bastille, the royal prison and symbol of despotism. A revolutionary committee was set up to rule Paris. In the provinces peasants broke into castles and destroyed records of the ancient feudal duties they resented. In the Assembly, a decree was passed abolishing feudalism. On August 26 1789, a Declaration of the Rights of Man, influenced by the similar declaration in the US, proclaimed Liberty, Equality and Fraternity. Distinctions between the "estates"; nobles, clergy, peasants were removed. All classes were to be equal.

Revolutionary dress was adopted, of cap, sans-culottes (trousers rather than aristocratic breeches), and the red, white and blue cockade. All were now addressed as "citizen". Georges Danton, a lawyer, emerged as spokesman for the "sans-culottes", as the lower-class revolutionaries were called. Political clubs were formed, such as Danton's radical Cordeliers, and the Jacobin club of

Storming the Bastille: the mob is aroused by Desmoulins, and the castle is taken.

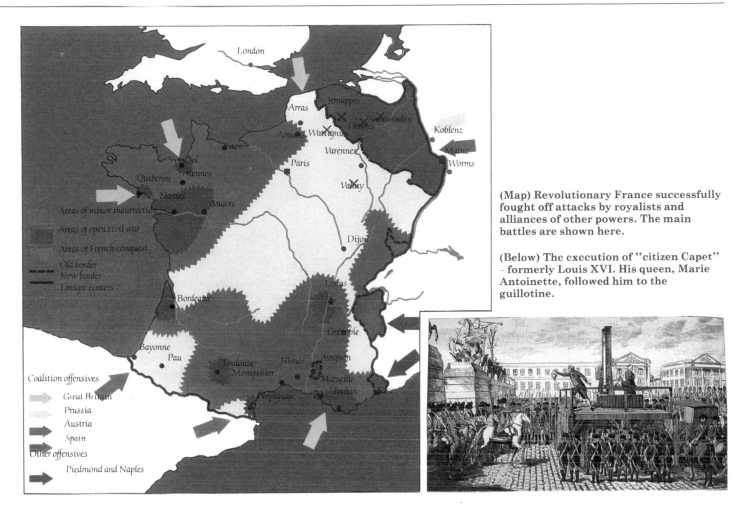

(Map) Revolutionary France successfully fought off attacks by royalists and alliances of other powers. The main battles are shown here.

(Below) The execution of "citizen Capet" – formerly Louis XVI. His queen, Marie Antoinette, followed him to the guillotine.

Robespierre and St Just, who saw themselves as the watchdogs of the revolution. The King, who had been forced to come to Paris by a mob of Parisian women, and had had to accept a limited monarchy, tried to escape. He was recaptured, and soon after, in August 1792, militants broke into the Tuilleries Palace and he was imprisoned. Encouraged by Jean-Paul Marat, mobs also broke into the prisons and massacred many nobles and clergy.

Many French nobles had fled from France, and they persuaded Prussia and Austria to try to destroy the revolution, and restore the King. This moved opinion against the monarchy. A republic was declared, and after a trial in which Robespierre spoke strongly against the King, now called Citizen Capet, he was guillotined. The guillotine was a dropping axe, designed by Joseph Guillotin to make execution painless.

A Convention was formed to make a constitution, and France was governed by the Committee of Public Safety, dominated by Danton, Robespierre and Marat. Danton was its first chairman, and played a leading part, with his inspiring oratory, in raising patriotic fervour to defeat invasions by Austria and Prussia, and royalist risings.

The radical Jacobins, known as the "mountain", from the high seats they had in the Convention, were able in this time of emergency, to oust the moderate Girondins. With the support of the Paris mob, they arrested and executed them. They were equally severe on atheists, led by Hébert. Danton was concerned at the increasing terror in the actions of the Committee, and left it to lead a moderate group, the Indulgents. Robespierre now dominated the Committee, for Marat had been assassinated. Robespierre was an austere, severe man, known as "the incorruptible", dedicated to the revolution, and determined to use coercion to destroy all oppositon. He used irregularities in Danton's affairs as Minister of Justice, to have him arrested and executed.

In place of Catholicism, Robespierre established the cult of the "Supreme Being", and the worship of reason. A new calendar was begun, with 1792 as Year 1, and new months of three ten-day weeks.

In July 1794, the Convention finally reacted against the Terror, in which 1,251 "suspicious persons" had been guillotined. Robespierre was arrested. He still had the support of the radical mob, but Robespierre, although he had been a dictator, wielded his power in the cause of the republic, and bowed to its authority. Instead of speaking to the crowd, he attempted to shoot himself. He failed, but not long after he followed his many victims to the guillotine.

Napoleon Bonaparte
1769–1821

Napoleon Bonaparte, Emperor of France (1804–14, 1815) was one of the world's greatest generals. His victories included Toulon (1793), Pyramids (1798), Marengo (1800), Hohenlinden (1800), Austerlitz (1805), Jena (1806), Wagram (1809) and Ligny (1815). Napoleon won control of nearly all Europe.

Napoleon Bonaparte was born in Corsica. He attended military school in France, where he was persecuted by other boys for his small size and foreign birth. He graduated 42nd in a class of 51. Napoleon joined the army as a lieutenant of artillery, and distinguished himself in command of the guns at the siege of Toulon, 1793. He was promoted to Brigadier-General in recognition, at the age of 24.

Napoleon was sympathetic to the French Revolution (see pages 70–71), and friendly with Robespierre and the radical Jacobins, and when they fell from power, he was left friendless and under suspicion. However, in October 1795, he commanded the troops that successfully defended the National Convention and the republic against a royalist rising. In gratitude the new French Government, known as the Directory, gave him command of the French army in Italy. In 1796, he married Josephine de Beauharnais, a connection which strengthened his political position.

Napoleon showed his genius in the campaign in Italy. He used rapid movements to cut his Austrian enemies' armies in half, so that he could then destroy them piecemeal. He was 60 miles (100 km) from Vienna when the Austrians sued for peace. He had won at least 14 pitched battles during the campaign.

The ambitious Bonaparte next planned to cut the British route to India, their major colony, and landed in Egypt in 1798. Victory in the battle of the Pyramids put Egypt at his mercy, but his fleet was destroyed in the Nile delta by Nelson (see page 75). Bonaparte

returned secretly to France, to find the Directory in disarray after losing what he had gained in Italy. He saw an opportunity to further his personal ambition. Bonaparte took part in a coup in November 1799, which replaced the Directory with a three-man government, the Consulate, with himself First Consul, and effectively the most powerful man in France.

Napoleon introduced a wholesale rationalization and modernization of French government and law, vital after the chaos of the Revolution. He also created the Bank of France, and built many roads and bridges, mainly for military reasons. In 1802, Napoleon made himself Consul for life, and virtual dictator. In 1804 the Pope came to Notre Dame cathedral in Paris and celebrated Napoleon's assumption of the title of Emperor:

Napoleon took the crown out of the Pope's hands and crowned himself, to show he was subordinate to no one.

Napoleon extended his Empire by military conquests and alliances forced on nations cowed by his military genius. He was unable, however, to defeat Britain at sea. He organized Europe into the "Continental System" to exclude British trade, but this alienated some of his allies, including Russia. He put his own relations or his marshals in power in some of his satellite countries, and this also caused resentment, especially in Spain, where a revolt began in 1808. He also sacrificed his wife to his ambition;

An English cartoon showing the Russians "snuffing out Boney".
(Bottom left) Napoleon's crossing of the Danube before Wagram (1809).
(Below) Napoleon on his way to St Helena.

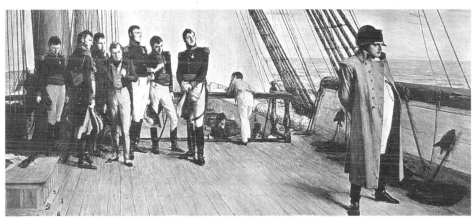

he divorced her in 1809 to marry Marie-Louise to forge a connection with the Austrian royal house.

Napoleon invaded Russia in 1812. His Grand Army captured Moscow in September 1812, after a bloody battle at Borodino, but the Russians burned Moscow to deprive him of supplies and winter quarters. He was trapped. Forced to retreat, the Grand Army was destroyed by cold and hunger. Napoleon hurried back to Europe and raised a new army, but the quality of his troops was never the same again. He suffered a catastrophic defeat at the Battle of the Nations (Leipzig) in 1813. The armies of Russia, Prussia and Britain, led by the Duke of Wellington and the Prussian general Gebhard Blücher, were too strong for Napoleon's troops and in April 1814 he surrendered.

Napoleon was exiled, but only as far as Elba, off the coast of Italy. He retained the title of Emperor. He escaped in February 1815, and when he landed in France, the army flocked to their old master. His triumph lasted only a hundred days. He beat the Prussians at Ligny, and two days later met the British at Waterloo (June 18 1815). The battle only swung against Napoleon when the Prussians arrived to reinforce Wellington's embattled troops.

Napoleon attempted to escape to the United States, but could find no ship able to break the British blockade. He appealed to the British for protection against Blücher, who had threatened to hang him. The British exiled him to St Helena in the Atlantic, where he died six years later. The Napoleonic legend lived on, and in 1840 he was buried with great pomp in Paris at the request of King Louis Philippe.

Horatio Nelson
1758–1805

Horatio Nelson was the most famous commander in the history of the British Royal Navy. He revolutionized naval tactics, and won a series of daring victories in the Napoleonic Wars against France and Spain, including the battles of the Nile (1798), Copenhagen (1801), and Trafalgar (1805), where he met his death. He had already lost an eye and an arm in battle.

(Above) Emma, Lady Hamilton. Nelson's affair with her caused much scandal, but did not lessen his popularity with the ordinary people. Emma lived in poverty after he died: their daughter became a schoolteacher.
(Right) Nelson's flagship at Trafalgar, the 100-gun *Victory*.

Horatio Nelson was born in Norfolk, the son of a country parson. An uncle of his was a captain in the Navy, and at the age of twelve he too went to sea. Nelson rapidly demonstrated an aptitude for sailing, but also a certain frailty of health. In 1775, he had to return from service in the Indian Ocean due to bad illness. This did not prevent his being promoted to lieutenant, and two years later, at the age of 21, he became the youngest captain in the Royal Navy. He served in the West Indies with distinction, but once again was invalided home.

Nelson had already demonstrated his qualities of leadership, and when Britain went to war with the French Republic, he was recalled to active duty. Nelson served in the Mediterranean from 1793, under the command of Admiral Hood, and lost the sight of his right eye when hit by flying splinters in action off Corsica in 1794.

Nelson was made a commodore in 1796, and Rear-Admiral in 1797. In that year, he passed undetected right through an enemy Spanish fleet. He reported its presence to his superior, Admiral Jervis, and distinguished himself in the resulting battle off Cape St. Vincent by capturing two Spanish ships. Later in 1797, Nelson had his right arm blown off in a raid on Santa Cruz.

Nelson showed his flair and tactical originality in the first of his great victories as commander of a fleet in 1798. He cornered Napoleon's fleet in Aboukir Bay at the mouth of the Nile, and by unexpectedly sailing between them and the shore he defeated and destroyed them, cutting off Napoleon's retreat from Egypt (see page 72).

Nelson, by now Sir Horatio and a national hero, took the news of his victory to the court of Britain's ally, the King of Sicily. There he met and fell in love with Emma, Lady Hamilton, the wife of the British envoy. Nelson had been married in the West Indies as a young man, and his affair with Lady Hamilton soon became public, and caused a scandal. However, their relationship lasted until Nelson's death.

In 1801, Nelson was made Vice-Admiral and posted to the Baltic Sea under Admiral Parker. Parker was a cautious man, quite unlike the dashing Nelson. At the Battle of Copenhagen (April 1802), when he was ordered to withdraw, Nelson put his telescope to his blind eye, and declared that he could not see the signal. He then proceeded to cripple the enemy Danish fleet. He was now created a Viscount.

Nelson was a brilliant and unconventional commander. He showed a high regard for the personal well-being of his officers and crew, and his leadership was characterized by a humane and sensitive attitude unusual for the time. In battle, he employed what became known as the "Nelson touch", giving great freedom to his individual captains to use their initiative under his overall tactical supervision. This usually meant plunging straight into the heart of an enemy fleet, disrupting its formation and destroying it in sections by superior firepower. Surprise and daring were at the centre of his method.

Nelson put his tactics to good effect at the battle of Trafalgar (October 1805). Nelson was commanding the Mediterranean fleet, in HMS *Victory*, under orders to keep the French fleet in Toulon. Eventually they escaped, and Nelson was able to bring them to battle. His 27 ships were faced by 33 French and Spanish ships, led by Admiral Villeneuve. Nelson ordered his ships to break the enemy line, and as they sailed into battle, hoisted the famous signal, "England expects that every man will do his duty".

The battle was a decisive victory. 18 of Villeneuve's ships were captured or destroyed. Napoleon's hopes of an invasion of England were finally dashed, for the Royal Navy was now supreme. However, England lost its great hero. Nelson was wounded by a musket shot early in the battle, as he stood on his quarterdeck. He made an easy target in his Admiral's uniform and medals. He died as the battle ended. Nelson was given a hero's funeral in London, and buried in a special place of honour in St Paul's Cathedral. HMS *Victory* survives, and can be visited in Portsmouth harbour.

(Bottom left) Nelson's death on the deck of HMS *Victory*. His dying words to Captain Hardy of the *Victory* were reportedly, "they have done for me at last."
(Bottom right) Nelson's death caused great shock in Britain, and he was given a lavish hero's funeral.

Arthur Wellesley, Duke of Wellington

1769–1852

The Duke of Wellington was one of the most distinguished British soldiers. He defeated Napoleon at Waterloo (1815). He was British Prime Minister, 1828–30.

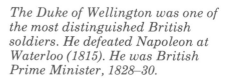

(Top right) The Battle of Waterloo; Wellington's greatest triumph, but, he said, a "close run thing". (Below) Wellington outside his headquarters at Mont St Jean, Battle of Waterloo.

Arthur Wellesley was born in Ireland, the fourth son of the Earl of Mornington. After attending Eton college, he spent a year at the French military school in Angers, where he mixed with French boys he was later to meet in battle. In 1786 he joined the army. He rose rapidly, for in seven years he was a Lieutenant-Colonel.

In 1796, Wellesley was posted to India,

and it was there that he first acquired a reputation as both a soldier and a statesman. For nine years he fought hostile natives in the hill country of central India, whose forces were far larger than his own. He was Governor of Mysore, and won a decisive victory at Assaye in 1803. He demonstrated his diplomatic skill in negotiating the treaty that ended the conflict. Arthur's brother Richard was British viceroy (governor), and together they brought the principalities of central and southern India under British control.

They both returned to England in 1805. Arthur became an MP, and pursued a dual career in soldiering and politics. At the height of the war against Napoleon, military service had to come first. Napoleon ranged practically the whole of Europe against Britain, but his placing of his brother Joseph on the throne of Spain provoked a revolt, which made the first hole in his Continental System. This gave an opportunity for the British to open a front in Europe. Wellesley commanded an army to Portugal, and beat the French General Juno at the battle of Vimiero (1808). His superiors allowed the French to withdraw, and for this they and Wellesley were recalled and tried by court-martial. Wellesley was cleared of any guilt.

In 1809, his successor, Sir John Moore, was killed at Corunna, and Wellesley resumed command, having persuaded the Government to maintain the front in Portugal. In the subsequent Peninsula Campaign (1809–14), Wellesley won victories over Napoleon's great marshals; Soult (Talavera, 1810) and Masséna (Bussaco, 1810). At Salamanca in July 1812 he defeated 40,000 French soldiers in 40 minutes. He also showed his diplomatic skills in his handling of relations with the Spanish guerrillas. Madrid and Barcelona were liberated, and by 1814, the French had been driven back over the Pyrenees mountains. The drain on Napoleon's resources caused by the Peninsula War was a major factor in the Emperor's defeat.

Wellesley was created Viscount of Wellington in 1810, and Duke in 1814 in recognition of his achievements. He resumed his political role as envoy to the Congress of Vienna (1814–15), which was intended to reorganize Europe. He returned to the battlefield hurriedly after Napoleon escaped from Elba. At Waterloo on June 18 1815, these two great generals at last met. The result was victory for Wellington (see page 73).

Wellington became a member of the Cabinet, and attended further diplomatic congresses. As Prime Minister (1828–30), he tenaciously opposed a growing movement for parliamentary reform and extension of voting rights. His house was attacked by stone-throwing mobs, but the stubborn duke would not retreat, or even recognize that the cause of reform should be taken seriously. This mistake brought the fall of his government.

Wellington fought a duel while still Prime Minister. The Earl of Winchelsea accused him of favouring Catholics and betraying the Church of England, and Wellington demanded the right to "satisfaction"; a duel. When it took place, both shot wide, and the whole affair was both a fiasco and a scandal, since it involved the leader of the nation risking his life. Wellington's public reputation was tarnished by these events, but only for a few years.

Wellington was a man of iron discipline, but he was not a cruel or hard man, and the nickname of "iron duke" commonly attached to him was given only after his death. His soldiers, whom he called the "scum of the earth", knew him as "Nosey", because of his large nose. In his old age, however, Wellington was venerated as the "Great Duke".

(Below) Wellington addressing the House of Lords. He continued to serve in government after being prime minister, and even after he retired, his advice continued to be sought.
(Bottom) Wellington's funeral procession. He was buried in a place of honour under the dome of St Paul's.

Chaka
c.1773–1828

Chaka founded the Zulu Empire in southern Africa. He brought 50,000 people under his rule, and created a fearsome fighting force.

When Chaka was a boy, the Zulus were a small clan of the East Nguni-Bantu people, living in what is now Natal, South Africa. Chaka lived a fatherless childhood, amongst a people who despised his mother, and who finally threw her out of the village. As a youth he served brilliantly in campaigns for Dingiswayo, chief of the Mtetma. In 1816, he was sent by Dingiswayo to be chief of his own clan.

Chaka ruled with an iron hand, meting out instant death even to trivial offenders against his will. Under his rule, the Zulu tribe was transformed. He built an army of warriors, called *impis*, on a regimental system distinguished by shield-markings. They were armed with a short stabbing-spear, the *assegai*. Previously, clan warfare had been fairly bloodless; on meeting, the weakest tribe gave way before there were many casualties. Chaka's men fought to conquer or exterminate, and their new weapon forced close and bloody combat. The remnants of enemy tribes would be incorporated into the Zulu tribe. He developed a new battle formation, con-

Cetewayo, a successor of Chaka, surrenders, 1879.

sisting of the "chest" and two "horns". The horns would encircle an enemy held by the strong chest. Behind the chest was the "loins"; a reserve who sat facing away from the battle to keep them from getting excited and leaving their position before they were ordered by the *indunas*, who directed the battle with hand signals.

Chaka subdued, destroyed or scattered all surrounding tribes, forcing a great migration of peoples away from the area, called the *Mfecane* or "Crushing". The Zulus became all-powerful; all that remained of those that did not join them were smoking villages. Dingiswayo was murdered. The people who had made Chaka's life a misery as a boy were impaled on their own fences.

In 1827, Chaka's beloved mother died, and he went berserk. Over 5,000 Zulus were immediately slaughtered, and all pregnant women were killed, along with their husbands. No crops were planted for a year, and cows were killed so that even calves would experience the loss of a mother. His men finally revolted in 1828. His half-brothers Dingane and Mhlangana murdered him. He left the Zulus masters of a vast part of South Africa, and disruption over a much wider area.

Simon Bolívar
1783–1830

Bolívar, known as "the Liberator", was a Venezuelan soldier and revolutionary, who led the Spanish colonies in the northern half of South America in their fight for independence. He liberated New Granada (Colombia) and Venezuela (1821), Ecuador (1822), Peru (1824) and Upper Peru, now Bolivia (1825). He is a revered historical figure.

Bolívar was the son of a Venezuelan aristocrat, and an unruly child. By the time he was nine, both parents had died. At the age of sixteen, he went to Europe to complete his education. After three years in Spain, he returned in 1801 with a Spanish wife, who died almost immediately from yellow fever.

Bolívar's response to this tragedy was to throw himself into politics, although still very young. He went back to Europe, where the idea took root that he must liberate his country from Spanish rule, and he took a vow to achieve this on Monte Sacro in Rome. Bolívar was present at Napoleon's coronation in 1804, and was deeply impressed by Napoleon's demonstration of what one

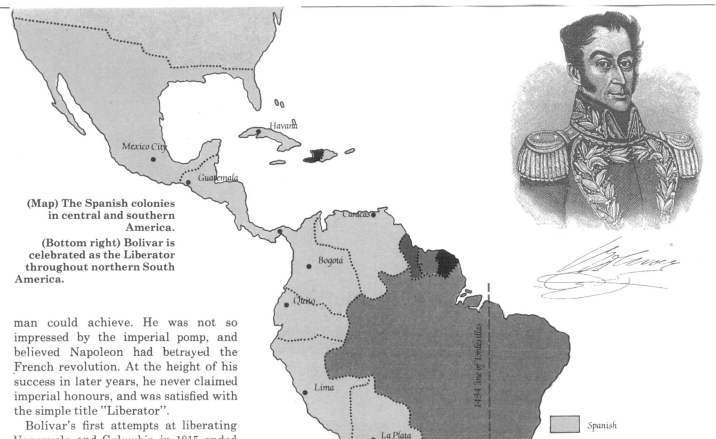

(Map) The Spanish colonies in central and southern America.

(Bottom right) Bolívar is celebrated as the Liberator throughout northern South America.

Spanish

Portuguese

British

Dutch

French

man could achieve. He was not so impressed by the imperial pomp, and believed Napoleon had betrayed the French revolution. At the height of his success in later years, he never claimed imperial honours, and was satisfied with the simple title "Liberator".

Bolívar's first attempts at liberating Venezuela and Colombia in 1815 ended in defeat by Spanish royalist forces, after initial success. Bolívar sought refuge in Jamaica, and returned to the fight in 1818, with a force of British volunteers. This time he raised an army in the interior, made a daring crossing of the Andes mountains, and caught the royalists by surprise by arriving from an unexpected direction. He freed Venezuela and Colombia, and the following year extended his control to Ecuador. Royal forces were forced back into Peru, where Bolívar followed them in 1824. He linked up there with the liberator of the south, San Martin, a modest unassuming man, who relinquished his forces to Bolívar. In 1825, Bolívar's achievement was completed by the conquest of Upper Peru, which renamed itself Bolivia in his honour.

Bolívar was a man of great vision and strength of character which outweighed defects of temperament that sometimes caused him to be cruel and violent, and at other times to be depressed by failure. Bolívar dreamed that South America would be united together in a confederation that would make it a force in the world. Bolívar himself became an internationally-known figure, but he was unable to counter the divisive national feelings in the new republics. Bolívar's attempts to impose his ideas by dictatorship failed, and Bolívar died a disappointed man, preparing to leave for Europe.

Bolívar's achievement was, however, monumental, and he is revered today as the founder of South American independence.

Simon Bolívar el Libertador

Abraham Darby

1678–1717

Abraham Darby revolutionized the production of iron at the beginning of the 18th century. His ironworks played a crucial role in the Industrial Revolution.

If any place can be called the starting point of the Industrial Revolution, it is the village of Coalbrookdale on the river Severn in Shropshire. It was there that Abraham Darby perfected a process that made possible some of the key inventions and products which sparked the great movement towards industrial production in England in the 18th century, and which brought in its wake a complete change in the British way of life. People left their villages and their work in agriculture to join others gathered together in towns.

Abraham Darby was an iron maker in Bristol. Iron was traditionally made by heating the rock it came from (ore) in fires made from charcoal. The resulting product was too brittle to make either large heavy items or very delicate and intricate ones. It was also expensive, since it depended on wood supplies for charcoal, and timber prices were high as wood was much in demand for other purposes.

In 1708 Darby introduced a new method of casting iron, using sand rather than clay, which enabled him to produce ironware pots cheaper than those his competitors made in brass. Less wealthy people could now afford them, creating a large market for ironware. Darby's great innovation came in 1709. He bought up an old ironworks at Coalbrookdale, where he knew there were abundant supplies of sulphur-free coal (coke). Darby used this fuel in the new blast furnace he constructed. Coke could support a greater weight of iron than charcoal. It enabled him to make large quantities of iron of high quality, free from dependence on timber supplies. This led to increased production of iron at cheaper prices, and more than anything made industrial expansion possible.

Darby's high-quality iron was used to manufacture the first steam engines, invented by Thomas Newcomen, and its availability made the invention truly viable. By 1758, more than 100 Newcomen engines had been cast by the Darby works, now run by Darby's son, Abraham II (1711–63). Good and cheap iron made possible the invention and widespread use of the new machinery of

The Darby Ironworks. Coalbrookdale, Shropshire.

the Industrial Revolution. In 1779, Darby's grandson, Abraham III (1750–91) cast one of the world's first iron bridges at Coalbrookdale. In 1802 the works produced the first railway locomotive, to the design of Richard Trevithick. A museum now stands on the site.

Sir Richard Arkwright

1732–92

Richard Arkwright was an English inventor, who became one of the first modern-style industrialists. He pioneered methods which mechanized the spinning of thread and manufacture of cloth, using horse power, then water (1771) and finally steam (1790). His mill at Cromford, Derbyshire, was one of the first textile factories.

Arkwright was the youngest of the thirteen children of a poor Lancashire labourer. At the age of ten he was apprenticed to a barber in Bolton. For 20 years he earned his living in a cellar shop shaving working men at a penny a time. Eventually he became a hairbuyer and wigmaker. It was on his travels in this trade that a meeting took place that changed his life. In 1765, during a storm, he called at a cottage for shelter, and found James Hargreaves, spinning thread on a new loom he had devised called a spinning jenny. Hargreaves' invention could spin eight threads at a time. He used it in secret to prevent the idea being stolen. Arkwright persuaded him to share his secrets and was inspired to improve on what he had found, for Hargreaves' thread was too coarse for most uses. He spent long hours working on the idea, to the frustration of his wife, who more than once destroyed his experimental models, which she saw as a waste of time. They endured much poverty, and once a collection was made by his friends to replace Arkwright's tattered clothing.

Arkwright was not wasting his time, for in 1769, he succeeded in making an improved spinning jenny able to spin any number of threads, of any degree of fineness. Arkwright opened his first mill in Nottingham, powered by horses. Others soon copied his ideas, but Arkwright was a man of great talent, and by continual improvements and good business sense, he made a considerable fortune. His new mill at Cromford, powered by water, was a wonder of the age.

Traditionally, spinning was done in cottages, by spinners working irregular hours and producing thread of greatly varying quality. Unlike the jenny, Arkwright's new water-frame was too big for a cottage, and he brought all his workers under one roof. This was not the first factory, but Arkwright's was a model of cleanliness and order.

Arkwright was knighted in 1786. Even when he was famous, he still sometimes worked 16 hours a day. Other inventors took up his ideas; Samuel Crompton's mule (1779) and Edmund Cartwright's power loom (1785) were important innovations, but the most important was James Watt's steam engine, which liberated mills from dependence on river flows and fear of floods. The way was opened for really large scale production.

(Left) The bridge at Ironbridge, Shropshire, cast at Coalbrookdale.

(Right) Spinning by cotton mule. By bringing all workers under one roof, Arkwright ensured they all produced thread of uniform quality, and looms were active all year round.

James Watt

James Watt
1736–1819

Matthew Boulton
1728–1809

(Below) James Watt's first experiment with steam.

(Below right) The Soho Works, Birmingham, where Watt and Boulton developed and built steam engines for many industries.

James Watt made the steam engine the force behind the Industrial Revolution. He added many improvements to it, including the condenser, rotary motion and the flying ball speed governor. Boulton supplied a business brain to augment Watt's inventiveness and together they produced steam engines that could be used in every industry requiring power.

James Watt was born and raised in the fishing port of Greenock in Scotland. He was a delicate child, unable to attend school regularly, and was chiefly taught by his mother. He spent much time helping to repair nautical instruments such as sextants and compasses, and at the age of 19 went to London to learn instrument making as a trade. Ill-health cut short his stay, and after a year and a half he returned to Scotland to become an assistant at Glasgow University. There he met many scientists, including Joseph Black, whose theory of latent heat he was to apply to the steam engine.

The turning point in Watt's life came when he was given a model of a Newcomen engine by the science department to repair. Thomas Newcomen had built his "atmospheric engine" in 1705, using steam to push a rod through a cylinder, which raised a beam. This engine was used in mines for pumping water, but was not very efficient, for it used much steam to give little power. Watt saw this and set to work to improve it.

One Sunday, while out walking, Watt hit on the idea of using a separate condenser to cool the steam, and a steam jacket to keep the cylinder hot all the time, saving much precious energy previously lost in cooling. He also saw that steam expanded, and that this meant the cylinder need only be half filled with steam, the rest of the work being done by expansion. Watt was inspired both by Black's heat theory and his own observation of the power of steam as a child, when, he would watch the pressure of steam build up under the

Watt's ultimate steam engine; his improvements to Newcomen's original concept were so many that Watt is regarded as the father of the steam engine.

lid of his mother's kettle, and force its-way through the spout. In 1769, Watt was granted his patent, for "a new method for lessening the consumption of steam and fuel in fire engines". The amount of power from an engine dramatically increased.

The engine was still only useful for pumping, and from 1766 to 1774 Watt earned his living not from steam engines but as surveyor of Scottish canals. By 1774, he was bored with this job, and distressed by the death of his wife. He moved to Birmingham, and struck up a fruitful partnership with Matthew Boulton.

Matthew Boulton was a Birmingham industrialist, and a key member of the Lunar Society, a group dedicated to the advance of science and the arts in Birmingham and the Midlands. Its members included many of the important figures of the Industrial Revolution, such as Josiah Wedgwood, whose pottery factories dominated the world china

markets, and Joseph Priestley, a prominent radical philosopher and scientist, who discovered oxygen. Boulton was first interested in Watt's work when he was looking for a power source for his metal goods factory. Boulton was a talented engineer in his own right, and possessed a sharp business sense, which Watt lacked. They made a perfect combination for 25 years. Boulton suggested many of the improvements that Watt's technical skill made practical.

It was only after Boulton and Watt joined forces that the full potential of Watt's invention was realized. In 1776, they installed two industrial engines; one pumping water out of a mine, the other air into blast furnaces. Between 1781 and 1790 Watt added many improvements. In 1782 he doubled efficiency by making the piston push as well as pull. Boulton suggested a rotary motion, and Watt responded with the "sun and planet" gear. The steam engine could now drive a wheel as well as a beam.

The markets Boulton foresaw in cotton and malt mills soon materialized. By 1790, when the pressure gauge and centrifugal governor were introduced, enabling precise control of the engine, Boulton and Watt had made a fair fortune, and their engines were operating in paper, flour, cotton and iron mills, distilleries, canals and waterworks, and even in the manufacture of coins (Boulton's idea). The steam engine became the basis of the Industrial Revolution.

The two retired after 1794, leaving their sons to run the firm of Boulton and Watt. Watt travelled widely, and continued inventing in his retirement. His achievements were honoured by membership of the Royal Society (with Boulton) and the French Academy of Science. He was offered a baronetcy by the British government, but refused it out of modesty. He and Boulton were buried alongside each other in Birmingham.

Queen Victoria

1819–1901

Victoria was Queen of Britain 1837–1901, and Empress of India, 1877–1901. She reigned longer than any other British monarch. She gave her name to the Victorian age, the time of Britain's rise to imperial greatness in India and Africa, her leadership of the world in trade and industry, and great achievements in art, especially in architecture and literature. Under Victoria, the monarchy achieved new popularity, and it completed its development into a constitutional monarchy, not involved in politics or the business of government, a move which ensured the survival of the British monarchy.

Victoria succeeded her uncle, William IV, at the age of 18. She took her job very seriously, and was carefully taught the practice of it by her first Prime Minister, Lord Melbourne, who acted as a father-figure to the inexperienced young Queen.

Melbourne's place as Victoria's confidant and advisor was taken in 1840 when Victoria married her German cousin, Prince Albert of Saxe-Coburg-Gotha. Victoria and Albert enjoyed a settled, happy and conventional family life. They had nine children, whose marriages linked the British royal family with most of the Protestant ruling houses of Europe. Victoria was devoted to Albert, and he exercised a strong influence on her conduct of her job as Queen. He understood and accepted the constitutional position of the monarchy, as did Victoria, and they were careful not to interfere too much in

(Centre) The Crystal Palace.
(Above) The Industrial Revolution.
(Right) Four generations; Victoria with the future George V, Edward VII and Edward VIII.

politics. Their exemplary family life and dignified political attitude successfully raised popular estimation of the monarchy, tarnished during the reigns of George III and George IV.

When Albert did intervene in national affairs, most often in foreign policy, his contributions were usually wise and helpful. In domestic affairs, he promoted the arts, and was responsible for the display of British industrial and artistic achievements at the famous Crystal Palace Exhibition of 1851.

Albert received the official title of Prince Consort in 1858. Victoria was devastated three years later by his death. She retired into mourning in Windsor Castle, leaving it only in the summer months when she travelled to Balmoral, the house Albert had built for her in Scotland. Victoria disappeared from public life for many years. The popularity of the monarchy once again declined, and it was only the persistent persuasion of Benjamin Disraeli, one of her favourite prime ministers, that brought her back into public appearances. Disraeli pleased her by declaring her Empress of India in 1877, and in her final years she was once again restored to people's hearts, as a mother-figure for the far-flung British Empire and the personification of British greatness. Her Jubilee (1887) and Diamond Jubilee (1897) were times of public rejoicing.

Victoria had her faults. She refused to allow her son Edward to take any role in public affairs, because of his frivolity and womanizing, of which she deeply disapproved. This only led him to continue such behaviour as he had nothing else to do. He ascended the throne at the age of 60 with no experience of government at all. Victoria had deep likes and dislikes regarding the politicians of her day, which she did not hide. She particularly disliked Lord Palmerston and W.E. Gladstone. She complained that Gladstone, one of the great British prime ministers, always addressed her as though she were a public meeting. On the other hand, she was very attached to Disraeli. However, she always adhered to the rule of not becoming involved in politics, with the result that the monarchy was never damaged by political scandals, as happened frequently in Europe at this time. This is one of the major reasons for the survival of the British monarchy.

The Victorian age spanned a time of great change. Britain, now lit by bright electric lamps, spanned by a vast network of railways, was a far different place to that of 1837 when Victoria came to the throne. The British Empire was extended into Africa. It included territories on every continent so that Britons claimed that the sun never set on the Union Jack. Wars were fought in the

Life in prosperous mid-Victorian Britain: Derby Day at the Epsom races.

colonies, but Britain, secure behind a large navy, remained at peace, and became the world's most prosperous nation.

The Victorian age is also known as a time in which prosperity existed along-side great poverty, deprivation and misery amongst those who worked in the factories. These factories were the basis for Britain's wealth. Men, women and even children worked long hours for low wages and lived crowded together in conditions of appalling squalor. The disgrace of this situation was publicised by men like Lord Shaftesbury and the novelist Charles Dickens, and some slow progress was made towards reform.

Progress was also made towards political equality; most adult men were given the right to vote, regardless of wealth, in 1867. Women still had no vote.

The Queen died with the turn of the century, one of the best-loved of all British monarchs.

CANALS, ROADS, BRIDGES

John McAdam
1756–1836

Thomas Telford
1757–1834

Road layers in London, 1838. Road layers were a common sight after the introduction of the road surface perfected by McAdam and Telford (below).

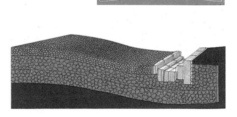

John McAdam and Thomas Telford were highly talented engineers, who started the use of a solid and reliable road surface, capable of taking heavy loads. Telford was very versatile, and apart from roads built harbours, tunnels, canals and bridges. His greatest achievement was the suspension bridge over the Menai Straits in Wales. McAdam and Telford revolutionized transport in Britain, making travel and the movement of goods, both easier and faster.

The Industrial Revolution created a vast amount of new traffic on Britain's roads, carrying raw materials to the factories from the mines and the ports, and the finished goods to the markets. Britain's existing roads could not cope with this traffic. Except in rare places where the magnificent Roman roads still survived, their surface was little better than mud. The wheels of carts over many centuries had created deep ruts, which would be filled, if at all, with loose stones. This merely made the journey even rougher. By the reign of George III most main roads had turnpikes, barriers erected at intervals at which travellers had to pay a toll to pass. These tolls paid for the upkeep of the roads, but until Telford and McAdam, techniques for improvement were very poor.

One answer to the problem was canals. From 1750 until about 1850, a great network of these artificial rivers was built across England. These canals were great feats of engineering, embodying tunnels through hillsides, and locks to enable them to rise above sea-level.

There was still a great need, however, to improve the roads. Stage coaches had begun to operate as early as 1659, and people wished to travel farther and faster as the commercial life of the nation increased with the trade produced by the new industries. In 1750 the fastest journey to Edinburgh from London by coach was 11 days. After the

McAdam's system (right) supports heavy traffic while allowing water to drain away. Otherwise roads would become quagmires (below).

efforts of the road-builders, this was cut to only 46 hours in 1830.

The first advances were made by John Metcalf (1717–1810), a colourful character, known as "Blind Jack of Knaresborough", who had lost his sight at the age of six, and had been a smuggler and stage-coach driver before becoming a road-maker. He emphasized the importance of foundations and drainage in building a good road surface, but his activities were limited to the north of England.

The name most associated with the dramatic improvement to Britain's roads on a nationwide scale is John McAdam, and rightly so. McAdam was largely self-taught as an engineer, but approached the subject in a scientific fashion.

McAdam was born in Scotland, but went to America at the age of 14, and made his fortune in commerce in New York City. He returned in 1783, and settled in Bristol, a great trading centre. He soon became interested in improving the roads that carried goods to Bristol. By 1810, this had become the dominant interest in his life, and he used up his fortune on experiments to find new and better surfaces. In 1827 his work was recognized by a Government grant of £10,000 and the post of Surveyor-General of London Metropolitan Roads.

McAdam introduced precision and method to road-building. He aimed to make a firm road that would withstand heavy loads, and which by good drainage would not be rutted or washed away by the rain. He started with a layer of shaped granite pieces, and then covered them with specially selected and graded granite or small stones. These would fit snugly together. The centre of the road was higher than the edges, so that water would run away to ditches at either side. This method of roadmaking is called "macadamized" in his honour, and with the addition of ashphalt is still in use.

Telford developed a similar method of road-making, though he used a deeper foundation, called the Telford base, which rendered his roads the longer lasting. By 1815 there was some 1,000 miles (1,610 km) of highway built with Telford and McAdam's methods. Their success was due in large measure to their careful

Thomas Telford

The years 1780–1830 saw many remarkable feats in transport engineering in Britain. Shown are the 970 yard (887 metre) Islington tunnel in London (1819), and the Irwell Aqueduct (1793).

organization and administration. They demonstrated that simple materials and unskilled labour were sufficient if used efficiently. The collection of stones by villagers was regularized, and the sight of men, women and children by the roadside breaking stones to the required sizes was a familiar sight in 19th century England.

Telford was the son of a poor Scottish shepherd, and was a shepherd himself, until he had taught himself enough to become first a stonemason and then an architect and civil engineer. His genial disposition was well-renowned; in his youth he was known as "Laughing Tam". Telford's first great work was the Ellesmere Canal in Shropshire, begun in 1793. He followed with two aqueducts carrying water over the Dee and Ceriog valleys in Wales; attracting national attention with his use of cast-iron troughs. He went on to develop communications in the Highlands of Scotland, building the Caledonian Canal, harbours at Dundee and Aberdeen, and over 900 miles (1,450 km) of roads, with 1,200 bridges.

Telford built many roads in England, distinguished by their well-designed gentle gradients, and that from Carlisle to Glasgow was considered the finest built at the time (1816). He designed and constructed the St. Katherine Docks in London, canal tunnels, and many bridges.

Telford made great use of the newly available material, cast-iron, for bridges, and was daring in his designs. His Menai Straits bridge (1819–26), linking Anglesey with the Welsh mainland, was 580 feet (177 metres) long, and was the first modern suspension bridge. Chains of wrought iron were towed across the water, hung from the towers at either end, then the roadway was suspended beneath. It lasted until 1940, when it was completely rebuilt. Quality and durability particularly distinguished Telford's work in every field.

Cecil Rhodes

1853–1902

Cecil Rhodes was the leading British imperialist of the late 19th century. He extended British colonization north from the Cape of Good Hope, and brought Bechuanaland (Botswana) and Rhodesia (Zimbabwe, Malawi and Zambia) under British rule. He was involved in the events that led to the Boer War (1899–1902), which resulted in the incorporation of the Boer republics into British South Africa. He gained a great fortune from diamond mining.

Cecil Rhodes (second from left) at the time of the Matebele wars (1896).

Cecil Rhodes was the son of an English vicar, but left England in 1870 because of poor health, and settled in South Africa with his brother Herbert. Rhodes quickly became involved in diamond mining in Kimberley. Life was hard at first for Rhodes, a rather eccentric introvert, who insisted on being known simply as "Mr Rhodes". He gradually became very rich, and by 1891 had acquired a controlling interest in the de Beers Company, which at that time produced about 90 per cent of the world's diamonds.

Rhodes had a great passion for the British Empire, and a dream to create a string of British colonies the length of Africa, "to paint the map red" from the Cape to Cairo. He also dreamed of uniting the British with the Boers, the tough Dutch settlers who lived mainly in Natal and Transvaal, and even of reuniting the United States with the British Empire. His two interests, diamonds and imperialism, combined to give Rhodes a great interest in the lands to the north of the British area of settlement in Cape Colony. In 1887, he obtained a royal charter for his newly-formed British South Africa Company to colonize north of Transvaal.

Rhodes' ambition to open up the African interior lands was blocked by two obstacles; Paul Kruger, the Boer leader in Transvaal, and Lobengula, King of the Matebele. Rhodes tackled Lobengula first, for he hoped that there were rich mineral deposits in his lands. Lobengula was very distrustful of the whites, and feared, rightly, that if he let them in, then he would never see them leave. He would only admit missionaries, but this was his undoing, for Rhodes used the son of one of these to act as his emissary, and to persuade the king to sign a treaty of friendship in February 1888. Lobengula hoped he had only given the whites the right to dig holes, but he had effectively signed his kingdom away.

Rhodes attracted much support in Britain, not least from Queen Victoria, to whom his ideas appealed. He also helped his cause by his intention to develop the territories at his own expense. The result was that the charter Rhodes was given had no fixed northern border. This left him free to press north of the Zambezi river, to found the town of Salisbury (now Harare), and to establish the colonies that were later called Northern and Southern Rhodesia, in his honour, in the lands of the Mashona and the Matebele.

Rhodes became prime minister of Cape Colony in 1890. He was successful as an administrator, and initiated the policy of setting land aside for the exclusive use of the Africans. There was trouble in the north, however, resulting in the defeat and death of Lobengula in war in 1893. Rhodes ordered the settlement of Matebeleland, and when this was approved by the British in 1894, he had reached the pinnacle of his success.

However, there proved to be little gold or diamonds in Rhodesia, unlike Transvaal. Rhodes became engaged in a plot against Kruger, which resulted in a raid on the Transvaal led by a close friend of Rhodes, Dr Leander Starr Jameson in 1895. The Jameson raid was a fiasco, and Rhodes was forced to resign all his posts in the Cape.

The British government took over the administration of Bechuanaland and the Rhodesias, but Rhodes remained active there through his company's interests. It was there in the Matopo hills that he chose his burial place, on a site known as the View of the World. He gradually returned to politics, and influenced the British High Commissioner, Milner, to take his view that Kruger was a menace. The antagonisms between Boer and British that had been aggravated by

some of Rhodes' policies, but not entirely caused by them, brought war in 1899. During the Boer War, he was involved in the seige of Kimberley, and served with the rank of colonel. He died before the end of the war, from heart disease. At the time of his death he was at the centre of a scandal involving a foreign adventuress, who had forged his name on some bills of exchange.

The last stand at Modderfontein, September 1901. The Boer War saw many British setbacks before the final victory.

Rhodes was buried after a triumphal procession to Matopo. He left a large fortune, some of which went towards the Rhodes scholarships, which have enabled many Africans to be educated at Oxford University. Rhodes contributed much to the growth of the British Empire in Africa, but his dream was never achieved, and a new generation grew up which had a less aggressive view of the Empire.

**(Left) The Boer War: British troops arrive at Springfontein.
(Above) Jameson captured by Boers. The fiasco of Jameson's raid cost Rhodes the Cape prime ministership.**

Charles Darwin

1809–82

THE LION OF THE SEASON.

ALARMED FLUNKEY. "MR. G-G-G-O-O-O-RILLA!"

Punch magazine pokes fun at Darwin's theory of man's descent from apes.

Charles Darwin was an English naturalist, who was principal author of the Theory of Evolution. He gathered material on the voyage of HMS Beagle *(1831–36), and published the Theory of Natural Selection, in* The Origin of Species *(1859). The Descent of Man (1871) suggested that man had the same ancestor as the anthropoid apes.*

Charles Darwin came from two distinguished English families. His mother was daughter of the famous potter and industrialist, Josiah Wedgwood. His father was a successful physician in Shrewsbury, and son of Erasmus Darwin, a poet and naturalist and associate of Matthew Boulton and the scientific Lunar Society (see page 83).

Darwin was an average pupil at school. He earned the nickname of "Gas" from his schoolmates for conducting chemical experiments outside school. Darwin studied unsuccessfully in Edinburgh as a doctor, and then spent three fruitless years at Cambridge University training as a clergyman. There he came into contact with scientific men, and dabbled in geology and botany.

The event which changed his life was his appointment as unpaid naturalist on HMS *Beagle*. This ship set off in December 1831 on a five year expedition to survey South American, Australian and New Zealand coasts and islands.

At the start of the 19th century, scientific thought was based on the discovery by Isaac Newton of the ordered nature of the universe, and different forms of life were seen as fitting together in an unchanging and ordered mechanism. Some thinkers, including Erasmus Darwin, thought that life might have developed through gradual change, but they had no scientific evidence. It was this that Charles Darwin was to provide.

On the voyage out to the Pacific, Darwin read Lyell's *Principles of Geology* and this had a profound influence on him. Lyell showed that the earth developed by gradual processes, such as erosion and subsidence, which were still continuing. Darwin's own observations confirmed this theory, and Darwin was deeply impressed by this idea of gradual development. On his voyage, he filled up copious notebooks with his observations of the similarities of living animals with extinct ones known through fossils, and the similarities and differences between animals on continents and those on nearby islands. It was on the Galapagos Islands in particular, with their many unique species, that the great question came to him; how did animals become as they are?

Darwin believed species developed from simpler ones, right back to simple one-celled creatures. Others had suggested this, but Darwin was the first to face and solve the vital problem of how to explain the great variety of animals that had come from these ancestors, and to give a scientific theory of the process of development. After 20 years of working on the *Beagle* material, handicapped by ill-health caused by the voyage, Darwin eventually produced the Theory of Natural Selection. The theory was that the fittest life forms are likely to survive and have more descendants than the less fit. They would pass on their characteristics to future generations, whilst others less adapted to their surroundings would die out in the perpetual competition for space and food. In this way species would very gradually change in accordance with changes in their environment.

In 1858, when Darwin was finally preparing an essay on the subject, he was startled to hear from Alfred Russel Wallace, who lived in the Moluccas, that he had come to the same conclusion. When Darwin presented his theory, he freely acknowledged that Wallace had the same idea. Wallace in his turn generously conceded that Darwin deserved the most credit for his 20 years of work. The friendship that formed between the two was unusual for two rivals for the credit for a scientific achievement.

Darwin in fact cared little for fame, and was not personally offended by the violent criticism of his theory by many scientists and churchmen. His theory seriously questioned the view that the universe was unchanging and constant since creation. The gradual nature of evolution implied the Earth was much older than had been believed. Darwin caused further controversy when he put forward the theory that mankind was no exception to evolution, and shared a common ancestor with the apes. Darwin's two greatest books were *The Origin of Species by Means of Natural Selection* and *The Descent of Man*, in which his new theories were presented with meticulous scientific evidence.

Darwin lived happily with a large family in Down in Kent. Poor health meant he could usually work only four or five hours a day, but dogged persistence kept him at his task. Darwin's ideas have had a profound effect on modern thought in zoology, botany, and many other fields, where the idea of evolutionary development has been applied. Darwin was buried in Westminster Abbey alongside some of Britain's greatest people.

(Above) Illustration of a pampas cat (*Felis pajeros*) from Darwin's *Zoology of the Voyage of the Beagle*.
(Left) HMS *Beagle*, on board which Darwin made the observations that led him to the Theory of Evolution.

In the early part of the 19th century, the German-speaking peoples were divided into a number of states, many of them very small. The largest were Catholic Austria and Protestant Prussia. Bismarck was a Prussian aristocrat (*Junker*) and was a strong energetic man, keen on riding and shooting and with large appetites for food and drink. Bismarck had a sophisticated intellect, and great sensitivity regarding real or imagined enemies. He was a devoted believer in the absolute power of the monarchy, and despised democracy and liberalism.

His strength of character was evident from the start of his political career. He created a stir in 1851 by smoking in the chamber of the federal *Diet* (a form of parliament), a privilege reserved for Austrians. He planned to unify Germans under Prussian leadership, and was convinced that the Austrians, who themselves claimed leadership, would have to be excluded if Prussia and Protestantism was to dominate.

Bismarck became Prussian Chancellor (prime minister) in 1862, and from then on pursued this aim with dedicated ruthlessness. He declared that problems could not be solved by votes and speeches, but "blood and iron". From this he received the nickname, "Iron Chancellor". He used alliances and wars to isolate Austria, and draw the other German states into union with Prussia.

Prince Otto von Bismarck

1815–98

Otto von Bismarck was Chancellor of Prussia, 1862–71, and of the German Empire, 1871–90. He was responsible for the unification of Germany, which he built up into a centralized empire, with a strong army. A brilliant and ruthless statesman, Otto von Bismarck dominated European diplomacy for 28 years.

Austria was defeated in the Seven Weeks War in 1866.

Bismarck believed in using fear of enemies to draw the Germans together, and in 1870 used subterfuge to provoke a war with France. He altered a letter from his king, to read like an insult to Napoleon III of France, and war quickly followed. The efficient Prussian Army Bismarck had built up easily defeated the French. In 1871, in the Hall of Mirrors in Versailles, Bismarck declared the establishment of the new German Empire, the Second Reich, with the King of Prussia as the *Kaiser* (emperor). Bismarck was made a Prince of the Empire.

Bismarck skillfully created a network of alliances, which protected Germany, allowed her to shape European diplomacy, and preserved European peace. He was a conservative in domestic affairs and persecuted Catholics and Socialists.

Bismarck was always on the alert for rivals. Wilhelm II dismissed him in 1890, to control policy himself, and Bismarck spent the last years of his life bitterly attacking those he believed had betrayed him.

(Below left) The Franco-Prussian War, 1870–71: the peak of Bismarck's career.
(Below) The bombardment of Schelestadt.
Napoleon III and Bismarck discuss peace.

Karl Marx
1818–83

Karl Marx was a German philosopher and political theorist. He founded modern communism. His greatest works were the Communist Manifesto *(1848) and* Capital *(1867–83). Marx's ideas have been very influential since his death, and form the official doctrine of the Soviet Union and other communist states.*

Marx was born a Jew in Trier in the German Rhineland, but was baptised a Christian at the age of six when his father converted to further his career. At Bonn university Marx studied law, philosophy and history and it was the work of the German philosophers Hegel, Feuerback and Hess that influenced the development of his own philosophy.

From 1843, Marx was increasingly involved with groups opposed to the authoritarian government of the Prussian monarchy. He also developed links with French and German worker groups. As a result of these affiliations, Marx and his wife Jenny were forced to move from the Rhineland to Paris, Brussels and then to London.

In 1844, Marx met Friedrich Engels, and began a fruitful partnership that lasted the rest of his life. With Engels he joined the League of the Just (renamed the Communist League), for which they wrote the *Communist Manifesto*. When in England, he founded the International Working Men's League (the "First International"), and wrote his greatest work, *Capital*. This was unfinished at his death, and was completed by Engels.

From 1850 to 1864, Marx lived a life of largely self-imposed poverty in London, researching for his books. He would not take a job, apart from that of a correspondent for the *New York Tribune*. Marx was an affectionate father, but in the early years in London he jeopardized his family's health by forcing them to live in poverty by his refusal to "become a capitalist". He also had a love affair with the family maid. Engels, working in his father's factory in Manchester, was able to provide Marx with money, a refuge from creditors, and invaluable material on the conditions of industrial workers in a great industrial city. With Engels' help, Marx was financially secure after 1864.

Marx constructed a complete framework of ideas concerning the development of mankind within an industrial society. He believed the working class would inevitably be the final victor, both as controllers and creators of wealth and no one would profit by another man's labour. Marx was buried in Highgate cemetery in London, which is still visited by admirers.

(Top right) Russian postcard; "Liberty, Equality, Brotherhood". Revolutionaries march towards a new dawn.

(Right) Cartoon showing Marx bound to his press, symbolizing Prussian suppression of his work, 1843.

Lincoln was born on the American frontier in Kentucky, of poor and illiterate parents, who lived in a log cabin. They moved in 1816 to southern Indiana, where conditions were no better. The nearest school was five miles away, and the teacher was only able to teach reading, writing and arithmetic. Lincoln's mother died for want of medical attention in 1818. Abraham helped his father make her coffin.

In 1830, Lincoln left the backwoods cabin, with his possessions wrapped in a big cotton handkerchief, and headed to the nearest settlement, New Salem, Illinois, to make his way in the world. Despite his lack of education and rough upbringing, Lincoln was an intelligent, sophisticated man, who proved to be an exceptional public speaker. This was allied to great honesty and integrity. In New Salem, he turned his hand to many jobs, voyaging twice down the Ohio and

A slave auction in the pre-Civil War South.

Mississippi rivers to New Orleans, serving in a company of volunteers in a war against the Indians, keeping a store and working as a village postmaster.

He was a failure as a trader, but his particular gifts suited him for the legal profession, and he trained himself to pass the Bar examinations in 1836. He soon made his name as a barrister in the country towns of Illinois. He had already become active in politics, for he was elected to the state legislature in 1834 as a Whig party candidate, while still studying law and working in a shop. He served four terms, and went on to represent Illinois in Congress from 1847 to 1849.

From 1849 to 1854, Lincoln concentrated on building up his legal practice, and made a name for himself as a lawyer and orator. He became increasingly concerned with the slavery question. Black slaves were still kept in the states of the South, and a major political question of the day was whether this institution should be abolished, or con-

Abraham Lincoln

1809–65

Abraham Lincoln was the 16th President of the United States, 1860–65. Lincoln was opposed to slavery, and his election caused the southern states to seccede from the Union. Lincoln led the North to victory in the American Civil War, 1861–65, achieving the reunification of the US and the emancipation of the black slaves.

(Left) Lincoln with his generals at the battle of Antietam (1862). His presidency was spent almost entirely at war. Union generals were outmatched by those of the South such as Lee and "Stonewall" Jackson, until Lincoln promoted the unorthodox Grant to overall command.

(Above) The battlefield of Gettysburg (1863). Three quarters of a million died in battle in this destructive war.

versely whether the new states being created on the frontier should be slave-owning or free. Lincoln joined the new Republican Party, which was anti-slavery.

In 1858, Lincoln rose to national prominence in seven great public debates with Stephen Douglas, his rival as Republican candidate for the Senate and a man regarded as a possible future president. Douglas won the nomination, but Lincoln won most of the fame with the power of his oratory. He declared, "A house divided against itself cannot stand. I believe this Government cannot endure permanently, half slave and half free".

To Lincoln, the unity of the United States was always the most important matter, and unlike the extreme abolitionists, he was not committed to forcing the South to give up its slaves, only to stopping slavery spreading and to working for its gradual disappearance.

In 1860, he was the Republican candidate for President, and easily won the election. He was inaugurated on March 4 1861, and was immediately faced with the dissolution of the United States. He was to spend all his presidency, and the remainder of his life fighting to repair the Union. Seven of the Southern states, fearful of Lincoln's opposition to slavery, secceded even before his inauguration, and formed the Confederate States of America. Lincoln would not attack but said he would "defend, protect and preserve if attacked". He mobilized the Army, and the rest of the states ranged themselves on one side or the other. Against the advice of his Cabinet, Lincoln kept a garrison in Fort Sumter in South Carolina, and the Confederate attack on it precipitated the outbreak of the Civil War.

Lincoln's declared aim was "to save the Union, and not to save or destroy slavery". As the bloody and destructive war continued, so feelings built in the North against slavery, and on September 22 1863, Lincoln issued the Emancipation Proclamation, freeing the slaves and giving them the rights of full citizens.

Lincoln conducted the war with vigour and single-minded determination. In a great public address on the battlefield of Gettysburg on November 19 1863, and subsequently, he advocated reconciliation, not revenge; "malice towards none". Lincoln was re-elected in 1864, and saw the war to a successful conclusion. On April 9 1865 the great Confederate general, Robert E. Lee surrendered to his Union counterpart Ulysees S. Grant, but Lincoln was deprived of the chance to ensure peaceful reconciliation by his assassination only five days later while attending a play.

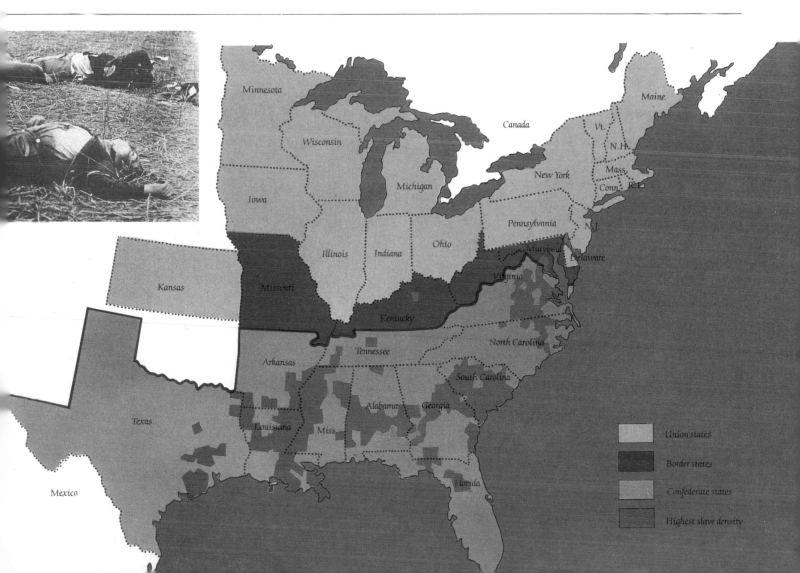

Union states

Border states

Confederate states

Highest slave density

THE MEDICAL REVOLUTION

Louis Pasteur
1822–1895

Louis Pasteur was a pioneering French bio-chemist and the first bacteriologist. He invented pasteurisation of milk, discovered bacteria are causes of fermentation, decay and disease, and developed vaccines for anthrax and rabies.

Pasteur was the son of a tanner from Dole, in Eastern France. He graduated from the École Normale in Paris, where the comment on his diploma for chemistry was "mediocre": possibly because his work was already too independent and original for his masters. He soon proved the judgment wrong, in a succession of university and college posts.

Pasteur's first discoveries came after he was asked by local wine producers to investigate why wine goes sour. He disproved the existing theory of "spontaneous generation": that things "went bad" because of the air. He demonstrated that it was the result of the activity of tiny organisms. These organisms (bacteria, or germs) were, he believed, like any other animals, and could be killed and prevented from breeding. He invented a process of killing them by heating, called pasteurisation. It was now possible to produce, preserve and transport wine, milk and beer without them becoming undrinkable.

In 1868, Pasteur was partially paralysed, but continued with his research. In 1881, he successfully came up with a protection for the deadly cattle and sheep disease, anthrax. He believed it was bacteria that also caused disease, and he isolated and cultivated a weakened version of those that produced anthrax. He injected this into 25 sheep, and some days later infected them and 25 others with the full disease. Only the 25 not treated died. This proved those injected had developed a resistance from their contact with the weakened germs that protected them against the full germs. Pasteur called the weakened viruses "vaccines" in honour of Edward Jenner, who had used cow-pox (Latin name, *vaccinia*) to protect against smallpox in a similar way.

Pasteur turned his attention to rabies (called hydrophobia in humans), and after painstaking research produced a vaccine from the bone-marrow of infected rabbits. He used this on July 6 1885 on Jacob Meister, a nine year old boy bitten by a rabid dog, and saved his life.

Pasteur created a revolution in scientific method, moving from the laboratory and tackling disease where it happened. He did not rest content with showing what caused disease, but sought to find solutions. He was a close friend of Joseph Lister, who applied his discoveries to the field of surgery. It was Lister who justly summed up Pasteur's achievement: "Truly there does not exist in this wide world an individual to whom medical science owes more than to you".

Pasteur was a practical scientist, doing most of his work in the field. Here he is trying out his rabies vaccine on a boy bitten by an infected dog. In such experiments with deadly diseases, Pasteur risked both his reputation and his life.

Lord Joseph Lister

1827–1912

Lister was a pioneering surgeon, whose discoveries were a crucial stage in the development of modern medicine. Lister was the first to devise methods to prevent infection during operations which resulted in the decline of patient mortality.

(Right) Lister's antiseptic spray, which filled the air with carbolic acid, sucked from a jar by steam.

(Below) Lister and his friend Pasteur honoured at the Sorbonne (University of Paris). Between them, their discoveries and innovations saved countless thousands of lives.

Joseph Lister was born of Quaker parents, and trained as a doctor at London University. He gained a reputation as an investigative surgeon, and rose fast in his profession, becoming Professor of Surgery at Glasgow University in 1860.

A major problem, which concerned Lister as a practising surgeon, was the large number of patients who died after operations. Many more operations were being carried out than previously, due to the invention of anaesthetic, but the death rate was in some hospitals as high as 60 percent. One third of all amputation patients died: and because of infection, amputation was often necessary even for fairly minor injuries. Part of the problem was that anaesthetic meant operations could be taken slower than before (though Lister could amputate a limb in 25 seconds) and this increased the risk of blood-poisoning and infection. It was still commonly believed that such infection was the result of "bad air", but in the light of Pasteur's discoveries (see opposite), Lister believed that the same micro-organisms that caused fermentation were to blame.

Lister was a working scientist, and he applied his theory in practice. He first concentrated on antiseptic measures (killing of germs), using a spray of carbolic acid, which was already used in treating sewage. The post-operative mortality rate fell in his wards from 43 to 15 percent almost overnight.

Lister was a great innovator and teacher. He designed new operating tables and tools, and drainage tubes for wounds. He saw that it was better to keep germs out altogether, and instituted white costumes rather than street-clothes for operating in, aiming to exclude germs from the operating theatre (asepsis). These measures were spread quickly amongst his own pupils, and other surgeons, whose attention was drawn by the dramatic success of his methods. Lister's pioneering work led directly to modern sterile operating conditions, which have saved countless lives.

The importance of Lister's work was obvious in the decline of patient mortality, and unlike some pioneers, his talents were recognised in his life-time. He was President of the Royal Society, 1895–1900, made a Baronet in 1883, and a Peer in 1897. His name is preserved in the Lister Institute of Preventive Medicine.

Florence Nightingale
1820–1910

Florence Nightingale, the "lady of the lamp", was the founder of modern nursing. She made important contributions to the improvement of military hygiene, and to the training of district nurses and midwives. She had considerable impact on modern hospital management.

Florence Nightingale was born of well-to-do English parents in the Italian city of Florence, after which she was named. At that time it was regarded as unthinkable that any respectable woman should enter a profession. When Florence, inspired by the miserable conditions she had seen in a hospital, said she wanted to become a nurse, her parents refused. Florence however was a woman of uncommon determination. Believing she had a mission from God, she trained as a

Florence would allow none of the nurses into the wards after eight at night, but would herself walk the four mile round with her lantern. (Below) The Charge of the Light Brigade, Crimea October 25 1854. Such actions sent hundreds of casualties to Florence's hospital.

nurse against her parents' wishes.

In 1853 she became superintendant of the Institute for the Care of Sick Gentlewomen in London, but found the work boring, referring to the place as "this little molehill". It was the outbreak of the Crimean War in 1854 that brought the challenge she craved.

The poor conditions of the military hospitals became a public scandal. Florence volunteered to go, and her friend, Sidney Herbert, the Minister for War, suggested she take a party of 40 nurses. They arrived at Scutari in Turkey on November 9 1854, to find the hospital rat- and flea-infested, and overcrowded with wounded, who were lying in the corridors on straw.

Florence met with prejudice and hostility from the doctors, who believed the wounded should be made to want to leave hospital as soon as possible, and who felt it was no place for women. Undeterred, she equipped her nurses with 200 scrubbing brushes, and introduced cleanliness and order. Burdened with administrative work, and with problems with her nurses some of whom had to be sent home for drunkenness or immorality, she still found time to give personal care to the patients. She knelt for eight hours a stretch dealing with wounds. Her regular round every night earned her the famous nickname, "the lady with the lamp".

Florence visited the Crimea to see conditions in the first aid stations, and became very ill with fever. She did not return home however, until the war was over. She found she had become a heroine in England, and twice met Queen Victoria, who encouraged her in her work.

From 1857 Florence was an invalid. She kept up a huge correspondence from her couch, driving her friends hard to achieve further improvements in army medical treatment, and in the training of nurses. Above all, she succeeded in overcoming prejudice to the extent that nursing became a respectable profession for women of any class.

Marie Curie
1867–1934

Pierre and Marie Curie, 1906.

Marie Curie was a Polish-born chemist, who worked in France. Marie Curie and her husband Pierre were a remarkable scientific team, who struggled for many years to discover the secrets of radioactivity.

Marie was born Manya Sklodowska, in Warsaw, Poland, which was then part of the Russian Empire. In 1891 Marie went to the Sorbonne in Paris, to study chemistry, living in poverty in the students quarter. In 1895 she married Pierre Curie, who worked with her in the university laboratory.

In 1897, Henri Becquerel, a colleague of theirs discovered mysterious emissions of invisible rays from uranium. Marie Curie devised the first method of measuring them, calling them radioactivity. She and Pierre searched for other sources, and came to the conclusion that pitchblende, the ore from which uranium is taken, contains two other radioactive elements. One they called polonium, the other radium.

The scientific world was sceptical, and the Curies struggled for four years to isolate enough pure radium to establish their case. Their equipment was primitive, their private laboratory a leaky shed, and the massive amounts of ore they required ate into their meagre finances. Finally in 1902 they had enough of the material, pale-blue with the phosphorescence of its radioactivity, to convince the world.

Pierre had turned down a professorship at Geneva to continue working with Marie: in 1904 he became Professor at the Sorbonne In 1903 the Curies and Becquerel were awarded the Nobel Prize for Physics. In April 1906, Pierre was run over and killed. This was a bitter blow to Marie, but she worked on, receiving the honour of being the first woman to teach at the Sorbonne when she was appointed to Pierre's professorship.

In 1911 Marie Curie won the Nobel Prize for Chemistry, for the discovery of radium and polonium; the first person to be honoured with two such awards. Subsequently, her work concentrated on the medical uses of radium in cancer therapy increasingly helped by her daughter Irène and Irène's husband, the brillliant Fréderic Joliot, who formed a research team like Marie and Pierre.

Aware of the dangerous potential of radioactivity in the wrong hands, Marie stressed the peaceful and beneficial side. She always freely published her results, for the sake of science, and gained no financial profit from them. She paid the ultimate price for her pioneering and selfless devotion to scientific study: she died in 1934 of leukaemia brought on by her prolonged exposure to radiation.

THE AGE OF THE RAILWAYS

George Stephenson
1781–1848

Robert Stephenson
1803–1859

George Stephenson made the first truly successful railway locomotive. He was engineer of the Stockton and Darlington railway (1821–5). His son Robert, also an engineer, was creator of the first generation of railway engines. He designed the famous Rocket *in 1829 for the Liverpool and Manchester Railway, which inaugurated the first commercial passenger railway services. Robert was also recognized internationally as a bridge builder.*

George Stephenson

Robert Stephenson

George Stephenson had contact with steam engines from his early childhood. His father was fireman of a colliery pumping engine in Wylam in Newcastle-upon-Tyne. The Stephenson family of six children shared one room in a cottage with three other families. George had no schooling, and went to work in the mine as a boy. He had a great desire to improve himself, and went to night school; he learnt to write his own name at the age of 19. To support himself and his wife, he did extra work, repairing shoes and fixing clocks, while a friend tended his engine. His studies earned him steady promotion. He became a builder of stationary engines at Killingworth colliery, earning enough to send his son Robert to school.

Stephenson's position gave him scope to experiment with steam engines. Collieries used horse-drawn wagons running on wood or iron rails. Many engineers were experimenting with the possibilities of steam power for this. The first to build a moving engine powered by steam was Richard Trevithick (1771–1833). He had developed a high pressure engine for deep mine use, and constructed steam powered carriages. In about 1802 he built a successful steam locomotive able to haul ten tons of iron at five miles per hour (8 kph). Its efficiency was reduced by Trevithick's use of a complex ratchet and cog system, because he believed, as many did, that smooth wheels would slip.

By 1812 it had been shown that smooth wheels and rails were usable. In 1813 William Hedley built *Puffing Billy* – so called because of the noise it made. It was used for colliery work in the Newcastle area. Stephenson produced an improved locomotive, *Blücher*, in 1814, and used it to haul coal nine miles to a seaport. However, it could not move any faster than a horse pulling a wagon.

Stephenson's next engine contained a crucial improvement. Exhaust steam was expelled through the chimney, which drew air into the boiler. This made the locomotive truly practical. Stephenson's *Locomotion No 1*, using this principle, and capable of 16 mph (25 kph), ran on the Stockton and Darlington Railway when it opened in 1825. This line was engineered by Stephenson and was the first railway to be designed for public use. It opened on September 27 1825, with a train carrying 450 people at 15 mph (24 kph).

George Stephenson surveyed and constructed the 40 mile (64 km) line between Manchester and Liverpool, begun in 1829. As well as engineering difficulties he had to face violent hostility from farmers who feared the new locomotives would frighten livestock. They were also concerned that horses would be replaced, and they would lose the market for the oats they grew. His *Rocket* won a competition to find an engine for this line in 1829, held at Rainhill. George Stephenson was now in great demand as a railway builder and consultant engineer, and he was able to live as a country gentleman.

Robert inherited his father's abilities and became a renowned engineer in his own right. He was manager and designer for his father's firm, and after the success of *Rocket* designed many other locomotives and set the standards for all others to be measured against. He introduced multitubular boilers in *Rocket* and later many other innovations.

Robert was also a highly talented civil engineer. His London to Birmingham Railway (1831–8) was a triumph in the face of great obstacles, and in its 112 mile (180 km) length included many engineering feats in tunnelling and bridgework. Robert Stephenson gained a world reputation as a bridge builder. He built the innovatory Britannia tubular bridge over the Menai Straits, and a six arch iron bridge for the Newcastle and Berwick Railway, using a steam hammer for the first time. He built railways and bridges in many parts of the world. Between them, the Stephensons ushered in the Golden Age of the railways.

Two Liverpool and Manchester Railway trains: (left) First class (above) Second class, with outside passengers.
(Below) The *Rocket*, designed by Robert and built by George's firm. In the Rainhill trials, *Rocket* attained a speed of 36 mph (58 kph). Both its rivals broke down.
(Bottom) George tending his engine. His father's assistant at 14, by the time he was 21 he was in charge.

Isambard Kingdom Brunel

1805–59

Brunel was probably the greatest engineer of the age of railway expansion. He was chief surveyor and designer of the Great Western Railway, 1833–46. He designed its terminus stations and bridges. (Paddington). He also made great improvements in steamship design.

SS *Great Eastern* laying the transatlantic cable. Although not a commercial success, like all Brunel's ships she introduced some important innovations, and did some useful work.

(Above) SS *Great Britain*. For many years she was a rusting wreck in the Falkland Islands.

(Right) Brunel's Clifton Suspension Bridge, His design for this bridge first brought him to prominence. Brunel's talents as a civil engineer were wide ranging. Some of his bridge designs for the Great Western Railway were revolutionary.

Isambard Kingdom Brunel was the son of Marc Isambard Brunel (1769–1849), a distinguished engineer. Marc was a Frenchman, who left France in 1793 during the revolution because of his royalist views. He lived in New York, and then in England. In 1825 he began work on an ambitious project; a tunnel under the River Thames using his new drilling shield. Isambard was educated in England and France, and then joined his father as a civil and mechanical engineer in 1822. In 1825, he was given the difficult and dangerous post of Resident Engineer on the Thames tunnel, although just 19.

The tunnel, from Wapping to Rotherhithe, was an exceptionally difficult project. The river broke through repeatedly, and on the most serious of these occasions, Isambard was badly injured. He spent his convalescence in Bristol, which was to be very important for the future course of his career. He found opportunities there for his engineering ambitions.

Brunel won a competition to design a bridge over the Avon gorge, in 1829; this was the Clifton suspension bridge, which took from 1831 to 1864 to build because of financial difficulties. He became known as an engineer of great promise, and in 1833 he applied to be chief engineer of the planned railway from London to Bristol.

He boldly told the selection committee that they were putting expense above quality, and that they would not get a good engineer, or a good railway, unless they were prepared to pay well. Surpris-ingly, the committee responded to this attack by selecting him. Brunel surveyed the whole route himself, usually on horseback, in ten weeks. He had to choose a route that passed through the important towns of Reading and Bath, but had to avoid steep gradients, for it was believed locomotives could not run up them. He also had to avoid antagonizing powerful landlords who might stop the railway being built.

Brunel was responsible for over 1,000 miles (1,600 km) of track, and designed all of the bridges and tunnels on the Great Western Railway, as it was called. These included the Box tunnel, with portals designed like medieval castles, and the Royal Albert Bridge at Saltash in Cornwall, which was 2,200 feet (670 metres) long, and carried the line 110 feet (33 metres) above the water.

Brunel designed the line for speed, and to achieve this wanted engines with extra large wheels. For this reason he adopted a broad gauge of 7 foot (2.13 metres), rather than Stephenson's 4 foot 8 inches (1.4 metres). This made the Great Western Railway unique in Britain. Brunel also turned to architecture, and designed the magnificent Paddington station in London, which is still much as he built it, a cathedral to steam as it has been described. The Great Western, the first section of which opened in 1838, was very much Brunel's creation, in every department.

Brunel's ships were equally epoch-making, but not always so successful. The *Great Western*, built in 1838, was the first wooden steam ship to cross the Atlantic. The *Great Eastern* was for a long period the largest ship afloat, and involved many improvements by Brunel to the steam turbines. Originally called *Leviathan*, it suffered a number of accidents, and was dogged with problems. It was a terrible financial loss, and anxiety connected with it probably hastened Brunel's death. In 1859, he was seized by a paralysing stroke while on board, and died ten days later. He left many monuments to his genius, including *Great Britain*, for long a wreck in the Falkland Islands, but now preserved in Bristol.

The famous "penny black".

Sir Rowland Hill
1795–1879

Rowland Hill was the originator of the modern postal system. He introduced the postage stamp, and a uniform rate for post within the United Kingdom, the "penny post". His system was adopted in 1840, and allowed great expansion of communication by post because of increased speed and efficiency.

Rowland Hill initially earned his living working on the tax system, and out of his ideas on taxes grew his great innovations in the postal system. Hill believed that the Government's tax income would increase as national prosperity increased and population grew, so that there were more people spending more money. He argued that to get more income, the tax-rate should therefore be low. Hill saw this principle had implications for the post. If more people could be made to use it, by reducing its cost, then its income would actually rise.

Hill set out his ideas in an influential book in 1837 called *Post Office Reform: Its Importance and Practicability*. At that time postage was paid in money either by the sender or receiver, according to a complicated scale of charges based on weight and distance. A letter within England could cost up to one shilling, and the average was six pence. The cheapest rate was four pence. The

system was expensive and time-consuming. Hill demonstrated that the cost of transporting a letter was an insignificant part of the cost of handling it, so that the scale of charges inflated costs unnecessarily. Instead he proposed a flat rate of one penny per half ounce, regardless of distance, since transit costs were just less than this. Payment would be made by the sender, who would affix an adhesive stamp showing the rate paid. There would be no need for the postman to collect the postage fee on delivery or the Post Office to keep complicated accounts.

Hill's idea caught the public imagination, although the Post Office was indifferent, and popular agitation caused the uniform rate penny post and adhesive stamp to be introduced in Britain in 1840. For the first time, sending letters was within the means of the ordinary people, and Hill's beliefs were more than borne out by the vast increase in use of the service, and in Post Office income. The new system was so simple, it was able to cope with the increased demand, and forms the basis for the modern system.

It took some time to catch on elsewhere. The first countries to try it were Switzerland and Brazil in 1843. Stamps were not adopted in the United States until 1847, and a single rate not until 1863. Street collection boxes were introduced in England in 1855, and in the United States in 1858. Rowland Hill was knighted for his pioneering ideas in 1860.

Alexander Graham Bell
1847–1922

Alexander Graham Bell was a Scottish-born physicist and inventor of the first workable telephone.

Bell followed his father and grandfather in researching teaching techniques for the deaf and studying the mechanics of human speech. After being taught by his family, he was educated at Edinburgh and London Universities. He became a teacher of music and speech. The strain of the work, and the shock of the death of his elder and younger brothers damaged his health, and his parents took him to Canada.

Bell began to lecture on his father's system of teaching sounds to the deaf, and in 1873 became professor of vocal physiology at Boston University. At the same time he was involved in long nightly sessions of experimentation, to the detriment of his health. Bell was no expert with his hands, and the delicate work was done by Bell's assistant, Thomas Watson, a model-maker. Funds came from the parents of two of his deaf students, George Sanders and Mary Hubbard. Bell married Mary, ten years his junior, in 1877.

The culmination of this work was the invention for which Bell will always be remembered. On March 11 1876, in a room in a Boston hotel, the first telephone message was transmitted, by Bell to his assistant. Bell applied for a patent, a confirmation that the invention was his, on March 14, just two hours before Elisha Grey did the same. Bell had to fight many court cases before it was acknowledged that he was indeed the first to construct and operate a telephone.

Bell's greatest invention was made before his thirtieth birthday, but Bell continued to invent to the end of his life, while maintaining his important activities as a teacher of the deaf. Not only did he make some useful further inventions, but he also encouraged young inventors, gathering a group of them around him. He was particularly interested in flying: whilst his own inventions were limited to man-carrying kites, some of his young friends, notably George Curtiss, played an important role in the early days of flight. Bell himself invented a device for locating bullets in bodies, and a type of waxed cylinder for Edison's phonograph. The invention for which he is always remembered, however, is his first, the telephone.

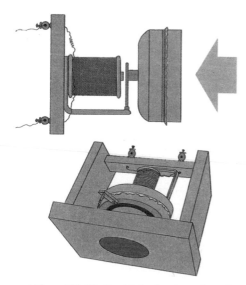

(Above) Bell's first telephone, using the same diaphragm for receiving and sending.
(Right) By 1900 complex telephone exchanges were common in the US and Europe.

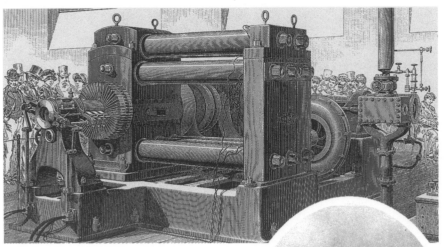

Thomas Edison
1847–1931

Thomas Edison was a prolific inventor, who had over a thousand patents to his name, Edison's most influential achievements were the phonograph and the electric light bulb.

Edison's great genius was his ability to apply other people's theoretical discoveries to practical, and sometimes revolutionary use. His own scientific understanding was modest. He had a great capacity for hard work; he defined genius as ninety-nine per cent perspiration and one per cent inspiration. He clearly however had great insight, as well as a good idea of what would be financially lucrative.

Born in Ohio, USA, Edison was a restless, inquiring boy. At the age of 12 he was a great success as a seller of newspapers, books and fruit on long distance trains, finding time to print a small newspaper at one end of the smoking car. This was the first newspaper made on a train. The enterprise ended when a chemical experiment he was making in the car exploded, and the guard threw him off the train at the next station. The

(Top) Edison's electric dynamo, 1881.

(Above) Edison, June 1888, with an improved phonograph, completed after five days' and nights' work.

Guglielmo Marconi
1874–1937

Marconi pioneered the development and use of radio, which has revolutionised communications throughout the world.

James Clerk-Maxwell predicted the existence of radio waves in his theory of electro-magnetism in the 1860s, and Heinrich Hertz first demonstrated their existence in 1887. It was Marconi, however, who had the vision to see how they could be put to practical use.

Marconi was the son of an Italian father and an Irish mother, brought up in Italy, and trained as a physicist. He experimented with the possibilities of electrical communication without wires, and with the aid of his own invention, the aerial, was able by 1896 to send a message $1\frac{1}{2}$ miles (2.4 km).

Marconi was unable to attract financial support in Italy, and came to England, encouraged by Sir William Preece, the chief engineer of the Post Office. He took out his first patent in 1896, and made rapid progress using kites and balloons to raise his aerials. In 1899 he sent a message from South Foreland in Kent to Wimereux in France, a distance of 31 miles (50km).

From the start, Marconi was aware of the commercial possibilities of his inven-

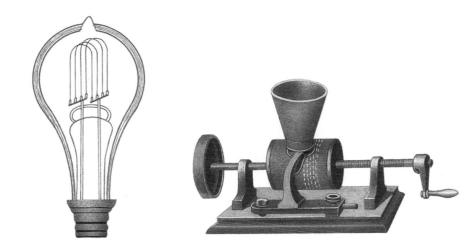

(Far right) Edison's mechanical phonograph. Sound was recorded onto tinfoil on a hand cranked revolving cylinder by a metal stylus.

(Right) Edison received over 1,000 patents for inventions and improvements. One of the most important was the light bulb. Observations of the behaviour of the current in the bulb, the "Edison effect", made possible the radio valve.

guard gave him a blow on his ear, which left him permanently deaf.

He later became a telegraph operator, and made his first fortune with improvements to a telegraph used to communicate stock-market prices, known as the ticker-tape machine. He was then able to set up a laboratory in New Jersey. He turned his attention to the telephone, and actually got a patent for a device for electrically transmitting voices a month before Bell and Grey, though his was not marketable as Bell's was. Edison did take Bell's invention and greatly improve it: Bell's company paid him $100,000 for the rights.

Edison's gramophone followed the next year, 1877. On November 29, after his workshop had made the machine he sketched for them, he shouted "Mary had a little lamb" into it, and to everyone's surprise the machine repeated it, with almost complete clarity.

The incandescent electric bulb had originally been invented by J. W. Starr of Cincinnatti in 1845, but it fell to Edison and the Englishman Joseph Swan to actually make it both a viable proposition and a worthwhile commercial investment. Edison used recent discoveries in vacuum technology and his own improvements to the generating system, which raised efficiency from 40 to 90 per cent, to produce a complete working electric light system, This was first marketed in 1880 by the Edison and Swan United Electric Company, and brought light into a world that had previously relied on candles.

Further inventions poured from the Edison workshop: dictaphones, megaphones and microphones. Edison made the crucial invention of sprocket holes in cine film, as well as a high speed camera and a projector, the "Kinetograph". He was involved in many squabbles over patents in this field, out of which he characteristically emerged financially better off.

Edison also experimented with electric storage batteries, though failing in the task of his final years, which was to find a battery driven car that would rival the gasoline powered automobile.

tions, and formed the Marconi Wireless Telegraph Company, which first specialized in installing radio in ships. Public attention was attracted when the Prince of Wales's yacht was equipped with wireless. The Prince was ill, and Queen Victoria was given daily bulletins of his progress by wireless.

The world remained sceptical however, until Marconi's greatest triumph, which was to send a message clear across the Atlantic from Poldhu, Cornwall, to Cape Breton, Nova Scotia, in December 1901. This caused an immense sensation in the civilized world. In 1910 he sent a message 6,000 miles (9,650 km) from Ireland to Argentina. A year earlier, he had received the Nobel Prize for Physics for developing radiotelegraphy.

Marconi's further developments included shortwave radio with a beam aerial, the basis for long-range broadcasting.

Marconi was honoured in Italy by being created a marquis, and represented Italy in 1919 at the Paris Peace Conference after World War I. In 1922 Marconi's company supplied equipment for the first commercial broadcasting services in London, which grew into the British Broadcasting Corporation (BBC).

Marconi showing his early apparatus to visitors, 1920.

VOTES FOR WOMEN

Emmeline Pankhurst
1858–1928

Emmeline Pankhurst was leader of the militant section of the British suffragette movement. Along with her daughters, Sylvia and Christabel, she made an important contribution to the winning of the vote for women in Britain.

Mrs Pankhurst is arrested after the suffragette attack on Buckingham Palace, 1914.

Women in the 19th century occupied a position of inferiority, and were denied many things that men had, merely on account of their sex. During the century, some brave and determined women won concessions in specific areas, such as the right to take university degrees, to become doctors, and the right to keep their property upon marriage. These gains, although important, each affected only a small section of the female population. The question of the vote was a cause that all women could see as relevant to them, and this is why it became the issue on which campaigners for women's rights concentrated their energies.

The vote was gradually extended to nearly all men by Acts of Parliament in

1832, 1867, and 1884. These changes were generally made by men who already had the vote. Women by and large had to fight their own battles; many preferred it that way as an indication of women's independence.

The subject of women's suffrage (the right to vote) was raised when the 1867 and 1884 Acts were discussed, and some MPs were in favour, but it was never seriously considered. Most men believed politics was a male affair. A quiet and orderly movement grew up, the National Union of Women's Suffrage Societies (NUWSS), led by a widow, Mrs Fawcett, but its campaign attracted little attention.

Emmeline Pankhurst founded the Women's Social and Political Union (WSPU) in 1903. She had worked on radical causes with her husband, Richard Pankhurst, and after his death in 1898, concentrated her interest on women's suffrage. Emmeline believed the NUWSS was not active enough to bring pressure to bear on politicians. Her daughter Christabel (1880–1958) convinced her that militant tactics were necessary. From the outset, therefore, the WSPU sought to make a nuisance of itself.

Emmeline's first tactic, demonstrations, marches and heckling at political meetings achieved nothing. After 1906 the WSPU tried more extreme measures, even law-breaking. Suffragettes chained themselves to lampposts, slashed pictures in public galleries and assaulted police. The driving force behind the escalating violence was Christabel, and it was decided that she should remain free, so she directed the movement from Paris. Emmeline remained in England, was imprisoned eight times, and wore herself to a shadow.

Failure to make real progress brought increasingly militant tactics, and a stronger response from the authorities. Suffragettes resorted to hunger-strikes to gain release from prison; after many got

Emmeline and Christabel in prison dress, 1908. Emmeline spent many spells in prison, severely damaging her health by hunger-strikes. Together they directed a campaign of increasing militancy and violence, in response to the intransigence of the authorities.

out this way, the Government used force-feeding. This aroused public outrage, and the Government then passed the "Cat and Mouse" Act under which it would release hunger-strikers and then re-arrest them. From 1912, the suffragettes became more desperate; buildings were set on fire and telegraph wires cut. One, Emily Davison, killed herself by throwing herself under the King's horse at the Derby in June 1913.

Emmeline's second daughter, Sylvia (1882–1960) was also involved in the movement, but concentrated her work amongst poor women in the East End of London. Emmeline and Christabel were a little snobbish and wished to appeal to better-off women, and when Sylvia refused to give up her East End women she was expelled from WPSU.

Public attention was drawn to the cause, in a way quieter tactics would not have achieved, but as the violence increased, it probably lost the movement some support. When Parliament voted on the issue, the margin was quite close, but was against women's suffrage.

World War I broke out in 1914, and Emmeline was released from prison where she was serving a three year sentence for arson. She advised women to become nurses and work in factories for the war effort, and it was this vital contribution women made in the conflict that tipped the scales. Women over 30 gained the vote in 1918, and those over 21 in 1928.

The women who fought for the vote did so as a step in the liberation of women and not because they wished to become involved in politics, for few of them remained politically active after the vote had been won. Emmeline lectured on hygiene in Canada after the war, and then became a Conservative party member. Christabel became a preacher in the United States. In 1936 she was made a Dame of the British Empire for her services to female emancipation. Sylvia remained a socialist and was a keen advocate of African independence.

THE AUTOMOBILE

Karl Benz
1844–1929

Gottlieb Daimler
1834–1900

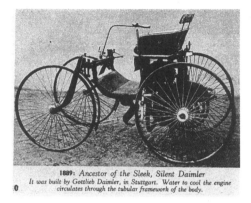

1889: *Ancestor of the Sleek, Silent Daimler*
It was built by Gottlieb Daimler, in Stuttgart. Water to cool the engine circulates through the tubular framework of the body.

Benz and Daimler were the most important pioneer contributors to the birth of the gasoline powered automobile.

(Left) Daimler's 1889 automobile. Springs were non-existent, and travel was distinctly uncomfortable. It was, however, a remarkable piece of engineering. (Above) Karl Benz. (Above right) Gottlieb Daimler. (Right) Just 20 years after the first car, they had become the height of fashion for the elegant and well-to-do.

He Is Certainly a Very "Chic" Gentleman, He Owns a Mercedes. 1908

Probably the first automobile in the world was Nicolas Cugnot's steam-powered tricycle of 1796. This was heavy and clumsy, as well as dangerous, and was not followed up. Others worked on a vehicle using petrol fuel, such as Siegfried Marcus in the 1860s, but the true pioneers of the modern automobile were Daimler and Benz, who saw the possibilities, and persevered where others had given up. Even in 1898, Marcus described the car as a "waste of time".

Benz and Daimler worked independently; in fact they never met, although their companies eventually merged (after Daimler's death). Benz was convinced to the point of obsession that the internal combustion engine invented by Niklaus Otto and Alfonse de Rochas would replace the horse and the new 'horseless carriage' would revolutionize transport. He was completely vindicated by events, but at the time, his friends thought him a little mad on the subject.

In the face of poverty and his friends'

derision, Benz persevered, and in 1885 he drove a tricycle driven by an engine fuelled by coal-gas round the cinder track outside his workshop, with his workmen running beside. He achieved a speed of 15 mph (24 kph). When he attempted a public showing, he forgot to steer and drove his car into a wall outside his house. The age of the automobile had however arrived; by 1888 he was employing 50 men in their manufacture, and in 1890 produced his first 4-wheeler.

Daimler was originally a gunsmith, who had taken up engineering and had worked with Otto on the internal combustion engine. Seeing more future in it for motive power than his employer, he

and his colleague Wilhelm Maybach started on their own. By 1885 they had built an engine capable of 900 rpm (Benz's could do 250 rpm). In 1886 they mounted it in their first 4-wheeled vehicle.

Daimler approached the question mainly from the starting point of the engine, Benz from the vehicle: at first Daimler merely envisaged the fitting of the engines in existing carriages. By 1890 he too was designing automobiles from scratch, as was his licensee Panhard in France. Many others followed the lead of these two pioneers in the 1890s, who had had the talent and the persistence to demonstrate the possibilities of the "horseless carriage".

Henry Ford
1863–1947

Henry Ford introduced mass production into the automobile industry. This enabled him to sell cars profitably at cheap prices and transformed the car from a luxury item to one within the reach of ordinary people.

The Model T Ford, or "flivver". For millions of Americans this was their first introduction to the freedoms of motor transport.

Ford worked as an engineer for a succession of automobile firms in the 1890s. He spent his spare time mending watches, and even when he was a millionaire, he enjoyed taking his friends' watches apart. Publicity from racing cars he had built enabled him to attract funds to set up the Ford Motor Company in 1903.

Ford's philosophy was different from other manufacturers, who saw the car as a luxury item, to be built by hand to customer's personal requirements. Ford wished to produce a car for the ordinary man: at once cheap enough for anyone to afford out of their salary, but built with the best materials and skills. In 1909, the first Model T, or "Tin Lizzie" as they were called, rolled off the assembly line.

Ford was not the first to use mass production, but he was the first to apply it to automobile manufacture, and he brought in many innovations. The simple design of his car allowed assembly in small stages, with each worker performing one task, as the assembly line moved past him at a comfortable waist-height. Ford recognised the monotony for workers of this conveyor belt technique, and in 1914 offered more than double the established wage, which caused such a rush for jobs that the police had to disperse the crowds with fire hoses. He took a paternalistic attitude to his workers; paying them high wages but not allowing them unions and insisting on their sobriety and thrift.

As he mastered the technique, so output increased, reaching a million in 1915, and the price, as Ford intended, fell. When production of the Model T ceased in 1927, over 15 million had been produced, and the price had dropped from $950 to $290.

Ford's character had many facets. He was a folk-dance enthusiast, collector of American historical artifacts, philanthropist and practical joker: a man who still enjoyed dirty engineering work but a ruthless businessman who built up a personal empire worth billions of dollars.

Ford more than anyone put America on wheels. There were drawbacks. Standardisation limited choice: "they can have it any colour so long as it's black." Ford fell behind some of his competitors in the 1920s because he did not recognize the increased demand for improvements by the motoring public he had created.

Henry Ford.

Orville Wright
1871–1948
Wilbur Wright
1867–1912

The Wright brothers were the first men to construct and fly a powered heavier-than-air aircraft. The first flight was made by Orville at Kitty Hawk, North Carolina, USA, on December 17 1903, and lasted 12 seconds.

For centuries man had dreamed of flying like the birds. By the end of the 19th century, men could ascend into the air using balloons, kites and gliders, but were always at the mercy of the wind. The invention of the internal combustion engine in the 1870s (see page 110) provided a power source for controlled flight, but the problem was to make it powerful enough to lift its own weight, and to design an aircraft to carry it. This problem was solved by the Wright brothers.

The Wrights were bicycle manufacturers in Dayton, Ohio in the United States. They were deeply interested in flight, and unlike many others approached the matter scientifically. They read all the books they could on the subject, and from 1899 to 1902 learned how to fly in kites and gliders before attempting powered flight. The key to their success was their methodical approach, supplemented by their engineering expertise, and the availability of tools and materials in their workshop.

The Wrights believed the major problem of flying a heavier-than-air craft was stability and control. They built themselves a wind tunnel to test their designs, and from 1900 tried them out at Kitty Hawk, North Carolina, where there were steady winds and sand dunes to cushion landings. There was no existing information on aerodynamics; their designs were perfected through trial and error. Having perfected a controllable glider in 1902, they moved to the next stage. There was no suitable engine available, so they built their own.

The Wrights' aircraft, called *Flyer 1*, took off after running on a wheeled trolley along a 60 foot (18¼ metres) monorail and landed on skids. The first attempt was made by Wilbur on December 14 1903, but the aircraft failed to take off. Three days later, at 10.35 am, Orville made it into the air, stayed aloft 12 seconds and landed safely. Later that day, Wilbur stayed airborne for 59 seconds.

In the next five years, the Wrights built more Flyers, and perfected techniques of banking and circling the craft. By October 1904 they had made 49 flights, some lasting 25 minutes. The world was slow to believe in their achievement; it took a trip to Europe and exhibitions by Wilbur in 1908 to convince Europeans that powered flight was now a reality. Wilbur died of typhoid in 1912, but Orville continued working on aircraft. Others improved on the invention, but all were building in some way on the research, calculations, and pioneering spirit of the Wrights.

The *Flyer*. The pilot lay on the lower wing beside the engine.

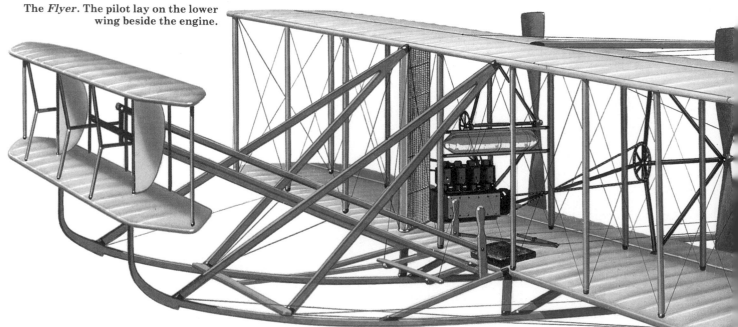

G. BOREL & Cie
25, Rue Brunel, PARIS

Louis Blériot
1872–1936

Amy Johnson
1903–41

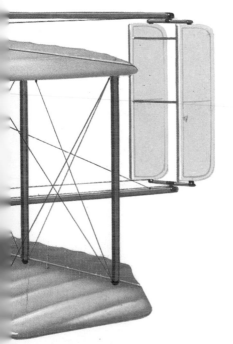

Louis Blériot was the first man to fly an aeroplane across the English Channel in July 1909. Amy Johnson was the first woman to make her mark in the history of flight. She flew solo from England to Australia in 20 days in 1930, made a record 10 day flight from London to Tokyo (1931), and a solo flight to Capetown (1932).

Louis Blériot originally made his fortune designing automobile lights. Blériot then devoted his fortune to building flying machines. He was inspired by the Wright brothers' demonstrations in France in 1908. He designed a number of very unusual aeroplanes, such as the canard, a tail-first monoplane. However, it was in a more conventional design that Blériot made his great achievement.

Blériot concentrated on monoplanes, unlike the Wrights who built biplanes. On July 25 he took off from Baraques near Calais in the *Blériot XI*, a mono-plane with a 28hp engine, and made the first heavier than air flight over the sea, crash-landing at Dover 37 minutes later. He won a prize of £1,000. Blériot went on to design many other monoplanes, with important innovations.

The great triumphs of distance and endurance, such as the Atlantic crossings of Alcock and Brown in 1919, and Lindbergh in 1927, were all achieved by men, until the remarkable English airwoman Amy Johnson. She was fascinated by flying after seeing a film in April 1928, and learnt to fly in the spare time from her office job. In December 1929, she was the first woman to receive a ground engineer's certificate. She was a keen mechanic, and never happier than when involved in a greasy repair job. She was a domineering, arrogant person, who preferred to be known as Johnny and treated as one of the boys, but she won admiration by her determination.

Johnson was determined to join in the race for flying records, and with great self-confidence, asked for support from the director of civil aviation, Sir Sefton Brancker. With his help, she bought a second-hand Gipsy Moth biplane, which she called *Jason*, and on May 5 1930, set off to fly alone to Australia. She was caught in a sandstorm in the Arabian desert; and later had to force-land on a Java sugar estate, where holes pierced in *Jason*'s wings had to be mended with sticking-plaster.

She arrived in Australia after 20 days, and became a national heroine. She kept herself in the news by further flying feats, and by a stormy marriage to another flier, Jim Mollison. He was not such a good pilot, and when Amy generously shared the limelight by allowing him to fly the last stage of a transatlantic record attempt, he ruined it by crashing the aircraft. The marriage was ended soon after. During World War II, she became a ferry pilot, and in January 1941 disappeared, having probably crashed into the Thames and drowned.

(Group photo) Freud (bottom left) with Carl Jung (bottom right) in 1908. Jung was Freud's most brilliant pupil, but came to disagree with many of Freud's conclusions. Freud was intolerant of criticism, and their friendship ended.

Sigmund Freud
1856–1939

Sigmund Freud was the founder of modern psychoanalysis. He developed original theories on dream interpretation and about the workings of the human mind and methods of investigation into mental disorders. Among his books were Studies in Hysteria *(1895; with Breuer),* The Interpretation of Dreams *(1895–99),* Beyond the Pleasure Principle *(1920), and* The Ego and the Id *(1923).*

Sigmund Freud was an Austrian Jew, who lived most of his life in Vienna. He was top of his year at high school, and went on to study medicine. This was not so much out of a desire to stop suffering as to study human nature. His photographic memory ensured him excellent grades. Freud went into general practice in 1882 so that he could have the money to marry, though poverty postponed his marriage until 1886.

Freud became deeply interested in mental disorders, particularly hysteria, and he demonstrated that some illnesses with physical effects have mental causes. At first he experimented with hypnosis to investigate these. He later developed different techniques such as free association of words, and the study of "slips of the tongue" to discover the inner workings of the mind. He also felt that dreams provided insight in this area.

Freud concluded from his investigations that there existed an unconscious area of the mind, the "sub-conscious", which was the root of all human behaviour. This was influenced by all experiences, especially those of early childhood, and one of his most successful techniques was to get a patient to relive these experiences in order to con-front reasons for abnormal behaviour.

Freud was a small man, but an imposing figure, bearded and possessing sharp, striking eyes. He attracted many pupils, who carried his ideas further. Freud had a reputation of being aggressive, especially towards critics. He tended to either love or hate people.

Freud's fame spread throughout Europe, and so controversial were his new theories that he was either revered or reviled. Today, although some of his ideas have been discarded, and others cannot be proved, his basic view of the role of the subconscious is accepted as the starting point for the examination of human behaviour.

Freud regularly smoked 20 cigars a day, and developed pains in his jaw as a result. He had 33 painful operations, without lasting relief. In 1938, he had to be persuaded to leave Vienna when the Nazis took over; although ill his commanding presence still prevented a mob smashing his home before he left. He moved to London, and died the next year.

Sir Alexander Fleming

1881–1955

Alexander Fleming was a Scottish bacteriologist, who in 1928 discovered the possibility of using the mould penicillin as an antibiotic. Fleming received a Nobel Prize for the discovery in 1945.

Penicillin was one of the most important medical discoveries of the first half of the 20th century. It was found largely by a happy accident, though its significance would never have been understood and exploited without the skill and knowledge of Fleming. Alexander Fleming was a Scot, who trained in biochemistry, and came to specialize in the study of bacteria; the micro-organisms in the atmosphere that Pasteur and Lister had shown were responsible for disease and infection (see pages 96–97).

Fleming began his research at St Mary's Hospital, London, and was a pupil of Sir Almroth Wright (1861–1947), who perfected a vaccine for typhoid. From 1919 he concentrated his work on finding an antibiotic substance which would kill germs but not damage the cells of the body. His work made little progress until 1928. During that year, Fleming made his great discovery.

Fleming used specimens of germs called "cultures", growing on special jelly, for his experiments. One day, he found that a mould had settled on an old culture of the germs that cause carbuncles and surgical infections, and that there was a clear circle where all the germ cells surrounding it had been killed. The mould was *Penicilium notatum* (from the Latin *penicillus*, a brush, which the fungus resembled). Further research revealed it to have great antibiotic qualities. The discovery was an accident, but would not have been made if Fleming was not on the look out for it.

Initially, penicillin was too impure and unstable to be put to practical use. Fleming worked with two pathologists, Howard Florey and Ernest Chain, to find a method of manufacturing a usable drug. It was only under the pressure of the Second World War that a successful method was worked out. Florey took the method of making penicillin pure and

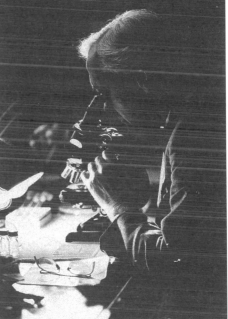

Fleming at work. He first discovered antibiotic substances in minute quantities in body fluids like tears. Having proved such substances existed, Fleming then sought a better and more plentiful source.

stable to the US, and freely gave out the secret to those who could make it. Manufacture of the drug soon followed, and it saved countless lives in the war, and has continued to do so since. Fleming. Florey and Chain shared the Nobel Prize for Medicine in 1945, in recognition of their life-saving work.

THE ATOMIC AGE

Albert Einstein
1879–1955

Albert Einstein was one of the greatest physicists ever. He laid down the General Theory of Relativity, and the principle of the conversion of matter into energy.

Einstein was born in Ulm in Germany, of Jewish parents. At the age of 15 he moved to Zürich. In 1901 he became a Swiss national. Einstein's first major discovery was made at the age of 26, when he was employed as a specialist examiner of patents in Berne. This was the Special Theory of Relativity, which revolutionized ideas of motion by demonstrating that all things are moving, and that a body's movement can only be measured against another moving body, that is, relatively. Einstein later went on to demonstrate that the measurement of time and space themselves is relative, because the person making the measurement is moving, and cannot be independent of them.

This brilliant young scholar was made professor successively at Zürich (1909), Prague (1911), Zürich again (1912), and Berlin (1913–33). It was at Berlin that Einstein perfected the General Theory of Relativity (1915–16). He also demonstrated that matter and energy could be made from one another, coining the famous equation, $E = mc^2$ (Energy is mass times the speed of light squared).

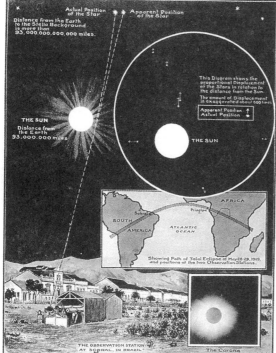

One of Einstein's many contributions to knowledge of the universe; the theory of the curvature of light by gravity.

Einstein honoured by his university for his achievements, March 1923.

116

This theory implied that if an atom, the basic unit of matter, could be split, great energy would be released. This is the basis of atomic power.

Einstein was forced to leave Berlin in 1933 because of Nazi persecution of the Jews. He settled in the United States, becoming a professor at Princeton in 1933, and a US citizen in 1940. He became increasingly concerned at the warlike purposes to which atomic energy could be put. In a famous letter to US President F. D. Roosevelt on August 2 1939, he warned of the danger to all people should the Nazis develop an atom bomb. It was this warning more than anything that prompted the great efforts made by US and British scientists during World War II to produce an atom bomb before the Germans. The bomb was completed and used twice in 1945.

Einstein continued to be fearful of atomic war and aware of his own part in the discoveries that made the bomb as well as the peaceful use of atomic energy possible. He urged, unsuccessfully, that the new United Nations organization should have control of atomic energy.

US Atom Bomb test, Bikini Atoll, July 25 1946.

Sir Ernest Rutherford
1871–1937

Sir Ernest Rutherford was a pioneering atomic scientist. He made crucial discoveries about the nature of the atom, showing it to consist of a nucleus and orbiting electrons. Together with John Cockroft and Ernest Walton he was the first to split the atom.

Ernest Rutherford was born near Nelson in New Zealand. He was educated in New Zealand, and then at Cambridge University. His first important atomic researches were made at McGill University, Montreal, Canada, and then in Manchester. He teamed up with the great physicist, Nils Bohr.

Bohr and Rutherford virtually created the science of nuclear physics by establishing revolutionary new concepts of the atom. The atom had previously been regarded as the basic particle of matter, and indivisible. Rutherford showed that the atom itself is made up of different particles, called ions, bearing either positive or negative electrical charges. There is a central nucleus, with ions called electrons orbiting around it. This theory was produced in 1910; Rutherford had already won the Nobel Prize for chemistry two years earlier.

In World War I, Rutherford was senior scientist in the British Admiralty working on submarine detection, a vital contribution to the war effort. After the war, in 1919, he became director of the Cavendish Laboratory in Cambridge, which under his guidance became the world centre of nuclear physics. It was there in May 1932 that Rutherford, with fellow-scientists John Cockroft and Ernest Walton, succeeded in the dangerous task of splitting the atom.

Rutherford's theories about the atom were proved. The great energy released, as Einstein had predicted (see opposite), showed the potential of the discovery. This was the crowning moment of Rutherford's distinguished career.

Rutherford was a great teacher as well as researcher, and taught many of the scientists who were to be involved in pioneering work on the atomic bomb and nuclear energy. Modern atomic theory is based on his discoveries. Rutherford was an inspired experimenter, with a happy knack of seeing the right step to take next. He was a warm and kindly man. Honours were heaped upon him; a knighthood in 1914, and the title Baron Rutherford of Nelson in 1925. He was buried in Westminster Abbey close to that other pioneering scientist, Isaac Newton.

Logie Baird
1888–1946

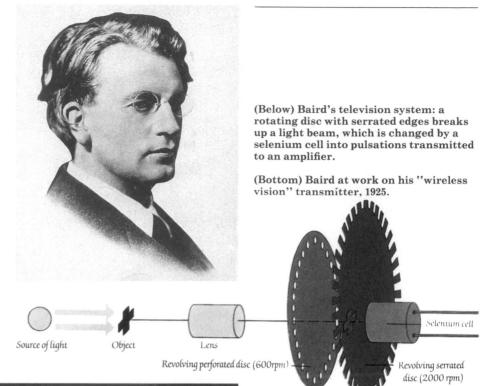

John Logie Baird was the first man to make a workable television system, in 1926.

Baird, a Scottish engineer, first began experimenting in the field of transmitting images of moving objects in the early 1920s. His first inventions were failures, and Baird was dogged by ill-health, but he was completely taken up with the aim of devising a means of transmitting moving pictures.

Success finally came in 1924, in a house in Soho in London. He managed to send a televised image over several feet. The method he used depended on mechanical scanning, using a fast moving spot of light (the flying spot). A

(Below) Baird's television system: a rotating disc with serrated edges breaks up a light beam, which is changed by a selenium cell into pulsations transmitted to an amplifier.

(Bottom) Baird at work on his "wireless vision" transmitter, 1925.

Source of light · Object · Lens · Revolving perforated disc (600rpm) · Revolving serrated disc (2000 rpm) · Selenium cell

revolving drum of some thirty mirrors, each tilted at a different angle, reflected the light from the object onto photo-electric cells, which changed light into electric impulses varying in strength according to the intensity of light. At the receiving end, these impulses controlled valves, which directed light onto another mirror drum, which reflected images onto a screen in a series of very quickly flickering spots.

In 1924, all that could be seen of the

objects he televised were outlines; by 1925 he could televise recognisable human faces. In 1926, he was ready to demonstrate his system to the world. He achieved lasting fame by giving the first public demonstration of a televised picture at the Royal Institution in London.

Baird went on to transmit the first pictures to a ship at sea in 1928, and in 1929 was granted a licence to develop a television service. The British Broad-

casting Corporation (BBC) gave him facilities to experiment, and when they began to transmit public television, the first in the world, in 1936, they used the Baird system.

However, another system had by this time been developed which used electronic rather than mechanical methods to scan an object. This was invented by Isaac Schoenberg, and was superior to the Baird system. The BBC used the two in parallel at first but switched completely to the electronic system in 1937. Although his method was superseded, Baird is remembered as the pioneer who demonstrated that television is possible.

Public television services were developed in Britain and the United States. In the United States the first broadcast was made at the 1939 New York World Fair; by mid 1940 there were 25 TV stations in the United States. Other countries did not have TV on a large scale until the 1950s. Television was still black and white in the early 1950s, though Baird had demonstrated colour TV as early as 1928.

(Left) A women's battalion of Red Guards, Petrograd, 1917.
(Below) Russian poster showing Lenin as father of the working people.

Lenin
1870–1924

Lenin was the leader of the Bolsheviks during the Russian Revolution in 1917, and founder of the USSR. Lenin was a major political theorist, adapting the writings of Karl Marx to suit Russian conditions. He has had a profound influence on the shape of twentieth century communism.

Vladimir Ilyich Ulyanov, who later adopted the name of Lenin to hide his real name from the police, became committed to revolution against the autocratic government of Russia at the age of 16, when his brother was executed for plotting to assassinate the Czar.

Lenin spent much of his life in exile. This began in 1895, when he was sentenced to three years in Siberia for membership of the Marxist Union of Struggle for the Liberation of the Working Class. On his return from Siberia, Lenin helped form the Russian Social Democratic Party. In 1900, Lenin publicly advocated revolution by the working classes to overthrow the Czar, and left Russia to escape the police. He lived in Germany, then Brussels, Paris, London, and finally Zürich.

Lenin believed that the working class had to be led by professional revolutionaries. Other members of his party believed they should simply work to improve the conditions of workers. At the party congress in London in 1903, Lenin won a close vote, and his supporters took the name Bolsheviks (majority men). The Bolsheviks subsequently organized themselves as a tightly-knit party.

It was their organization and discipline, and most importantly, the leadership of Lenin, that enabled the Bolsheviks to seize power in 1917. In March 1917, the Czar was deposed in the Russian Revolution, after three years of war had brought the country close to economic collapse, and the prestige of the monarchy had been ruined by scandals. A great deal of chaos followed, and Lenin, who had been brought back to Russia in a sealed train by the Germans, ordered his Bolsheviks to take over. They won support in the new "soviets" (workers councils) in Moscow and Petrograd (now Leningrad), and in November stormed the Winter Palace in Petrograd and overthrew the existing government.

Lenin immediately took Russia out of the war, making large concessions of territory to the Germans. The Bolsheviks had to fight hard to preserve the revolution and were not victorious until 1921. Lenin removed all political opposition and set up a one party state. He nationalized industry and agriculture and abolished private property. The hated Czarist secret police was revived to root out opposition.

Lenin was an idealistic man, who disliked the repression he felt forced to introduce to protect the revolution. He did not live long enough to relax it, for he suffered a series of strokes after 1922, and an assassination attempt in 1923 finally destroyed his health. He died in January 1924.

Mussolini with King Victor Emmanuel III.

Benito Mussolini
1883–1945

Benito Mussolini was dictator of Italy, 1922–43. He founded the Fascist party, and set up an authoritarian government, based on his own personal rule. He followed an aggressive foreign policy, and in 1940 joined World War II on the side of Hitler. He was overthrown in 1943, but was maintained in power by Germany in north Italy until the end of the war.

Mussolini was the son of a socialist blacksmith, and was himself a socialist revolutionary as a young man, In 1902–04, he lived in Switzerland to avoid army service in Italy, and became a journalist. On his return to Italy, he became established as a revolutionary journalist and a writer of cheap fiction. In 1912, he became the editor of the socialist newspaper, *Avanti*, but during World War I his political stance changed. Mussolini's nationalism increased, and he began to pose as a war-hero, though in fact he was wounded by his own side in grenade practice.

After the war, he became a leading opponent of socialism, and in 1921 founded the Fascist party. He was supported by businessmen and landowners frightened by the communist takeover in Russia. His gangs of blackshirted Fascists, known as Action Squads, broke up socialist meetings, and burned down union offices. They gained control of many cities in north Italy. The government did not have the will to stand up to Mussolini, and to many he seemed preferable to communism. He organized the "March on Rome" in October 1922, but he was invited to become prime minister by the frightened king even before the Fascists reached Rome.

Mussolini won great popularity in Italy by posing as a man of iron will, capable by his personality of solving Italy's problems, and restoring the greatness it had known in the days of the Roman Empire. He would never allow himself to be seen smiling in public. By 1925, backed by his backshirt thugs, he had become an absolute dictator, and called himself *Duce* (father). Mussolini modernized Italian industry and brought efficiency; for instance, he made the trains run on time. The Italians paid for this with the loss of personal freedom, and with an expensive and finally disastrous policy of territorial expansion.

Italy conquered Ethiopia in 1935, followed by Albania in 1939. Mussolini formed the Axis alliance with Hitler (see opposite), whom he admired, and joined in World War II in 1940. He invaded Greece, but there and in Libya, he had to be saved from defeat by Germany. The war was costly for Italy, and in 1943, after the British and Americans had occupied Sicily, Mussolini was deposed by members of his government. He was rescued from a mountain-top prison by a daring German commando raid, and was set up in control of north Italy by Hitler. When defeat was near, he and his mistress attempted to escape into Switzerland, but were captured by Italian resistance fighters, shot, and hanged upside down on butcher's hooks.

Planning the defeat of France, May–June 1940. The German *blitzkrieg* (lightning attacks) proved unstoppable.

Adolf Hitler
1889–1945

Adolf Hitler, leader of the Nazis, was dictator of Germany, 1933–45. World War II began with his invasion of Poland, September 1939. He conquered most of Europe, but was finally defeated in 1945.

Hitler was born in Austria. His ambition was to be an artist, but he failed to be accepted by the art college in Vienna, a fact which he blamed on the presence of Jews on the interview panel. He earned a living in Vienna, as a postcard artist and house painter.

By the outbreak of World War I in 1914, he was living in Germany, He served in the German Army during the war. He won a medal for bravery, although he never rose above the rank of corporal.

After the war, Hitler took up politics, and in 1921 was a founder-member of the Nazi Party. In 1924 he served a year in prison for plotting to seize power, during which time he wrote out his political ideas in a book, *Mein Kampf* (My Struggle). His ideas were a crude mixture of extreme German nationalism and racial bigotry. His particular hatred was directed at the Jews.

Hitler was a remarkable public speaker, and his ideas found a following at a time of poverty and unemployment, backed up by the bullying of Nazi thugs. After victory in the German election of January 1933, Hitler quickly made himself absolute dictator, calling himself *Führer* (leader). Potential opponents were murdered, sent to concentration camps or terrorized by the Gestapo (secret police).

The persecution of the Jews began in earnest in 1938, with the Crystal Night, when the broken glass of looted Jewish shops shone on the streets like crystal, Jews were forced to live in ghettoes, or were sent to concentration camps. In 1942, the "Final Solution" to the Jewish question was started – mass extermination in death-camps. By 1945, some six million had gone to their deaths.

Hitler began a policy of expansion. He occupied Austria in 1938, and Czechoslovakia in 1939. When he invaded Poland on September 1 1939, Britain and France finally decided to try and stop him. Poland, Norway, Denmark, the Netherlands, Belgium and France were conquered by the end of 1940, and Britain was only saved by the English Channel and her Air Force. In 1941, Yugoslavia and Greece were overrun and Russia was invaded. Hitler controlled most of Europe, and instituted a rule of terror. Races he regarded as "inferior", such as the Slavs, were persecuted and killed.

Hitler was finally defeated by a combination led by Britain, the United States and the Soviet Union. He spent the last weeks in his underground bunker in Berlin, and when it was obvious total defeat was near, he committed suicide.

Churchill sat in Parliament over 50 years. Shown here winning his seat in 1950.

Sir Winston Churchill
1874–1965

The victorious leaders of World War II: Stalin (USSR), Roosevelt (USA) and Churchill.

Winston Churchill was the British leader during World War II. He was Prime Minister, 1940–45 and 1951–55, and held many other major posts, including Chancellor of the Exchequer (1925–29) and First Lord of the Admiralty (1911–15, 1939–40). He was a fine public speaker and also a historian and painter.

Winston Churchill was the son of Lord Randolph Churchill and his American wife, Jenny. He did not distinguish himself at school, and was only able to get a place at Sandhurst military academy at the third attempt. He served as a lancer at the battle of Omdurman (1898), but found the routine of soldiering dull, and took leave to cover a rising in Cuba as a journalist. It was as a journalist that he saw much action in the Boer War in South Africa (1899–1902).

After that war, he entered politics, and though handicapped by a speech impediment that never completely left him, he rose quickly, first in the Conservative Party, and then as a Liberal, His career was never short of controversy. After four years at the Admiralty, preparing the Navy for the war with Germany, he was dismissed for the failure of the Dardanelles operation (1915), which he had hoped would end the war quickly. Churchill went to France, and fought as a soldier in the trenches. He later returned as a minister, and after the war switched parties again, and was Conservative Chancellor of the Exchequer, 1925–29.

Churchill was out of office in the 1930s. He was fearful of the growing might of Hitler's Germany, but his warnings were ignored. When war came, he was recalled to the Admiralty, and the message went around the fleet, "Winston's back!". In May 1940, amidst catastrophic defeats of Britain and her allies, he was chosen as the man to lead Britain to victory, and he became Prime Minister. France was defeated in June, and Britain was left alone to face Germany until the Ameri-

cans and Soviets came into the war in 1941. Churchill never disguised the seriousness of the situation, yet always managed to convey a confidence that Britain would win through. "I have nothing to promise you", he said on taking office, "but blood, toil, tears and sweat."

After the Battle of Britain was won by the few hundred fighter pilots of the RAF, he declared that "never has so much been owed by so many to so few." To Churchill this was Britain's "finest hour", and it certainly was Churchill's. He revelled in his role of war leader, taking an active part in directing strategy, and giving urgency to Britain's war effort. He forged close links with US President Franklin Roosevelt, and after the war believed Britain's future lay in the close partnership of Britain and the US, the nations of his parentage.

After the victory, in 1945, Churchill lost office, though he later served again as Prime Minister, 1951–55. He refused all offers of honours, except the knighthood pressed on him personally by Queen Elizabeth II. On his death, tributes were sent from around the world.

Charles de Gaulle

1890–1970

Charles de Gaulle was a French soldier, and inspirational leader. He led the Free French movement in World War II and was at the head of French forces when they marched into Paris in August 1944. He was head of the French government, 1944–46. He was called back in 1958 during a crisis. As President, 1958–69 he followed a strong nationalist policy. De Gaulle did much to restore French national spirit after the defeat in 1940.

Charles André Joseph Marie de Gaulle was a professional soldier, and graduated from the famous military academy at Saint Cyr. He fought with distinction in World War I, until wounded and captured in 1916. Between the two World Wars he became renowned as a master of the tactics associated with the new weapon, the tank, when most of his colleagues still concentrated on the horse. In 1940 he was made a Brigadier-general in charge of an armoured division. He

served as Under-secretary of Defence in the Government, and when the Germans overran France in June 1940, he went to London, where he declared himself leader of the free French. He was sentenced to death in his absence by the new French Government.

De Gaulle was strong-willed and highly patriotic, and his strident confidence that France would rise again was a great encouragement to the French people in their darkest hour. His allies, Britain and the United States, accepted him as head of the French Committee for National Liberation set up in Algiers, and as head of the provisional French

government set up after the D-Day landings in June 1944.

De Gaulle remained as prime minister for only two years, after which his dislike of the new French constitution caused him to resign. He remained in the political wilderness for 12 years, during which France suffered a series of political crises. It was as a result of a crisis in the French colony of Algeria, which threatened civil war in France, that the French turned again to de Gaulle. He became President under a new constitution, giving him great power, in December 1958.

De Gaulle dominated European politics during the 1960s. He made a historic reconciliation with the Germans, but in order to maintain France's leadership of Europe, he refused to allow Britain to enter the new European Economic Community (Common Market) in 1963. He built up France's armed forces, including nuclear ones, and pulled France out of NATO commands as part of a policy of asserting France's independence as a world power.

He restored the French economy, but restrictions on civil liberties provoked serious unrest in Paris in May 1968. De Gaulle's prestige was permanently damaged, and after a constitutional crisis the following year he retired.

(Far left) De Gaulle in London, 1940. De Gaulle rallied French morale after the French surrender to Germany and became the personification of French resistance.

(Left) De Gaulle voting in 1969. Defeat in the referendum on constitutional changes brought his resignation from the presidency.

A gathering of the remnants of the Communist Party after the Long March.

Chinese poster to demonstrate progress under the rule of Mao.

Mao Tse-tung
1893–1976

Mao Tse-tung led the Chinese Communist revolution, and from 1949 until his death he ruled China. He transformed his country, whose people had followed much the same way of life for 2,000 years, into a modern industrial nation. In China he is now venerated as a father-figure. His writings ranged from political theory to lyrical poetry.

Mao first became involved in politics in 1918, when he was a librarian at Peking (now called Beijing) University. Mao helped to found the Chinese Communist party, based on the teaching of Karl Marx, in 1921, and led an unsuccessful revolt in 1927 called the Autumn Harvest Rising. After his defeat he retreated to a distant country district. He was joined there by fellow communists after the party was outlawed and many of its members executed. They were constantly attacked by the forces of Chiang Kai-shek, the head of the Chinese Government.

In 1934 the by now huge group of 85,000 was forced to leave and set off on the famous Long March, In a journey of 6,000 miles (10,000 km) they crossed 18 mountain ranges and 24 major rivers. Many were killed by disease, starvation and fighting with Chiang, including Mao's two small children and his brother. When they arrived in Shensi, far to the North, a year later, only 8,000 men and 30 women had survived. During the Long March, Mao became undisputed leader.

In 1937 the Japanese invaded China and Chiang and Mao made a temporary truce to fight the invader. When the war ended in 1945, the tactics Mao had used to win the support of ordinary people, which involved giving them the land of rich landowners, enabled the communists to drive Chiang out of China.

They set up their own government in 1949 called the Chinese People's Republic.

As Chairman of the Communist Party, Mao now exercised complete control over the 7,000,000 people of China and was able to impose drastic reforms in farming and in industry. He called this the Great Leap Forward. Schoolchildren were made to learn the *Thoughts of Chairman Mao*, printed in a little red book.

In 1956, Mao's famous words "let a hundred flowers bloom" heralded a softening in official attitude to individual expression. Then in 1966 the "Cultural Revolution" gave power to the teenage Red Guards, who gave out harsh penalties to any who did not strictly follow Mao's ideas, especially those who still followed the ideas of Confucius (see page 11).

Mao became a god-like figure, a position he promoted, on one occasion proving his fitness by a well publicized swim across the Yangtse-Kiang, China's widest river. In his last years, power passed to his wife, Ch'iang Ch'ing, and her supporters, the "Gang of Four". After Mao's death they were ousted from power. The figure of Mao himself remained an example to all the people of China.

Tito at work. Tito developed from a partizan revolutionary to an internationally respected figure and one of the leaders of a new alignment of neutral independent countries.

Tito
1892–1980

Josip Broz, known as Tito, was leader of the Yugoslav communist partizans during World War II. From 1945 to 1980 he was head of the government of Yugoslavia. He is famous as the only leader of a nation in the communist bloc in Eastern Europe to assert his independence from the Soviet Union and survive.

Tito was born in Croatia, then part of Austria-Hungary, and fought alongside the Bolsheviks during the Russian Civil War, 1918–21 (see Lenin, page 119). He returned to his native land, which was now a part of the new state of Yugoslavia. He became a trade union organizer, and agitator for the illegal Communist Party. He spent six years in prison for these activities.

In 1941, the Germans occupied Yugoslavia, and Tito organized the National Liberation Front in the mountains of Montenegro to resist them. There was another resistance movement. led by Draza Mihailovic, a Serb and Minister of War in the royal government. Bitter rivalry arose between the two, but once it became clear that Tito's forces were more effective in fighting the Germans, he received the most aid from Britain and the United States, and was eventually recognized as leader. As a communist, Tito was also supported by the Soviet Union, and was able to make good his claim to be the country's ruler When the Germans retreated, Tito's Partizans were strong enough to liberate Yugoslavia before other foreign troops arrived, the only European nation able to do this.

This achievement gave Tito a wide range of support, even from those who were not communists. Tito became prime minister, and in 1953, president. He established a communist regime, with nationalized industries and collectivized agriculture, but reserved the right to decide what was right for Yugoslavia. The Soviet Union claimed to be the authority for all communist states, but Tito refused to obey. His popularity as a result of his role in the war, and his strident patriotism was such that he was able to defy the mighty Soviets. The Soviet leader, Stalin, declared that he could lift his little finger, and there would be no more Tito, but this was an empty boast.

Since 1948, Yugoslavia has followed its own path, maintaining good relations with the Western powers, whilst retaining a communist one party state. Some areas of Yugoslav life have been liberalized. Tito was a pioneer of the non-aligned movement of countries trying to keep out of any Soviet-American quarrel, and this is still Yugoslavia's position in international affairs. On his death, leaders from both East and West came to his funeral to pay tribute to a great national leader.

Mahatma Gandhi
1869–1948

Mahatma Gandhi was the driving force behind the achievement of Indian independence from British rule. He devised the new tactic of non-violent passive resistance and civil disobedience to win freedom. Gandhi united in his person the aspirations of all Indians, of whatever religious persuasion.

Mohandas Karamchand Gandhi, later known as 'Mahatma' ("saint", or "great soul") was educated in London, studied law, and became a barrister in Bombay. He practised law in South Africa, and it was there that he developed his ideas of civil disobedience and *satyagraha* (keeping true to the soul). He spent 21 years in South Africa, working to end oppression by the Transvaal Government of the Indian community there. He believed that freedom could not be achieved by force, both because it would provoke greater repression and because violence was bad for the well-being of the soul.

In 1914, he received assurances of better treatment from South African Prime Minister Smuts, and returned to India. In 1919, British soldiers fired on a demonstration in Amritsar, and killed 379 unarmed Indian civilians. This confirmed Gandhi's commitment to a non-violent solution. He gained control of the Indian Congress Party, and converted that party into a mass movement. In 1921, he promised that civil disobedience would end British rule within a year. A great wave of strikes, boycotts of British-made goods, refusal to recognize courts or pay taxes, followed.

The tactic did not achieve immediate success, but Gandhi was established as leader of the Indian independence movement. Gandhi was imprisoned four times by the British, but his methods were in the long run successful in causing the British to change their view of the Empire, and eventually to acknowledge the Indian right to independence.

Gandhi maintained his opposition to violence. When he felt the British were backing down on promises of greater freedom, instead of encouraging revolt he went on a long pilgrimage to the sea to make salt. The making of salt was a government prerogative, and this was a highly effective protest, even if it did put Gandhi back in jail. Gandhi was a man of great simplicity, who wore only a rough robe, went barefoot and spun his own cloth with the traditional spinning wheel. Such was his influence with the Indian people that in the final years of British rule he was able to halt violent and bloody communal rioting by fasting and refusing to eat again until the bloodshed ceased.

Indian independence was finally granted in 1947, but Gandhi did not live to enjoy it very long. On January 30 1948 he was shot and killed by a Hindu extremist, who resented Gandhi's acceptance of the division of India into two countries, India and Pakistan. Gandhi's spinning wheel became the symbol of the new India.

(Left) Gandhi at the time of one of his many arrests by the British.

(Below) Gandhi in 1925. His traditional spinning wheel symbolized the Indian way of life.

Martin Luther King

1929 68

Martin Luther King was a black Baptist preacher in the United States, who led the civil rights movement from the 1950s until his assassination in 1968.

The American blacks were given emancipation after the Civil War, in 1865 (see page 95), but continued to suffer from persecution and prejudice, especially in the former slave states in the South. After World War II, blacks began to press for equal rights. Martin Luther King emerged as the most important leader of the civil rights movement in the 1950s.

King came from Atlanta, Georgia, the heart of the South, and was the son of a Baptist preacher. He himself trained as a minister, and it was in his seminary

in Pennsylvania that he first read of Gandhi's ideas (see opposite). King was a deeply religious man, and Gandhi's non-violent approach appealed strongly to him. After taking a doctorate in Boston, King became a pastor in Montgomery, Alabama in 1954. In 1955, he became involved in a dispute that raised him to national fame. Blacks were forbidden to ride in the same buses as whites (segregation), and after a woman was arrested for defying this regulation, King organ-

ized a boycott of the city's transport system. Although his house was dynamited and his family threatened, King persisted until he achieved desegregation in 1956.

King was swept to the head of a national movement that successfully applied the tactics of boycotts, demonstrations and sit-ins in many other cities. In 1963, in Birmingham, Alabama, police used firehoses and dogs to disperse demonstrators against segregation at lunch counters, and this outraged many Americans. King was imprisoned, but continued to advocate non-violence. King won the support of white liberals as well as blacks, and over 200,000 people of all races met under the Lincoln Memorial in Washington on August 28 1963, to hear King's emotional declaration of his dream of equal justice for all.

President John F. Kennedy introduced civil rights legislation. He was assassinated before it was passed, but his successor, Lyndon B. Johnson, saw it made law. King was awarded the Nobel Prize for Peace in 1964, for his deep commitment to a non-violent, peaceful solution to injustice. He continued to campaign, attacking poverty, unemployment, and the United States involvement in the Vietnam War, as well as racism. King awoke the black masses, but was successful because he also attracted the support of many white people. However, some hated what he was doing, and in Memphis, Tennessee on April 4 1968, he was shot and killed. To demonstrate the simplicity of his cause, his cortège was a mule train.

COMPUTERS AND ROCKETS

Charles Babbage

1792–1871

Wernher von Braun

1912–1977

Charles Babbage was an English professor of mathematics. As well as a number of other inventions, he devised the basic principles of the modern computer, and devoted much of his fortune to perfecting it. Wernher von Braun was a German rocket engineer, who invented the V-2 rocket bomb. He worked in the United States after World War II and designed the Saturn V rocket that took men to the moon in 1969.

Babbage's first computer was built in 1827. It was called a "difference engine" and computed and printed logarithm tables, which Babbage had invented to aid mathematical calculations. His more complex "Analytical Machine" of 1834, would have been the world's first digital computer, with a memory and program-

Charles Babbage.

The V-2 Rocket – Hitler's "Revenge Weapon"; the first ballistic missile.

ming. The machine would have been steam-driven and very cumbersome, but Babbage was unable to get the finance to build it. He made use of an invention by a Frenchman, Jacquard, who used cards punched with holes to program a loom to produce patterned cloth. Babbage applied this principle to calculations, anticipating the use of programs in modern computers, first on punched cards, then on magnetic tape.

The actual construction of the computer had to await further inventions, and Babbage's machine was forgotten until his papers were rediscovered in 1937. Babbage's was an inventive mind in many ways: he also invented the locomotive cowcatcher and the speedometer, and played an important part in the establishment of the postal service under Rowland Hill (see page 104).

Wernher von Braun conducted small scale private experiments with rockets as a young man. These attracted the attention of the military authorities of Hitler's Germany. Financed by the Army, von Braun conducted important experiments, which finally resulted in the fearsome V-2 rocket, the world's first ballistic missile weapon, which was used by Germany in the last months of World War II to attack Britain. Von Braun was

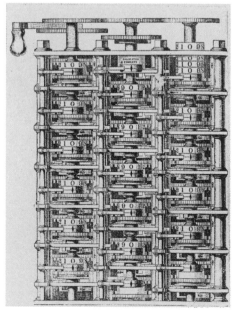

Babbage's complex "Difference Engine". He devoted his fortune to developing such machines. Some were too advanced to be built.

not a man of war, and was more interested in the peaceful application of his inventions – he was once arrested by the Gestapo because it was suspected he was devoting more time to developing his rockets for flights to Mars than as weapons of destruction.

At the end of the war in 1945, von Braun and his team surrendered to the Americans. They were taken to the United States, where their experiments were continued, first with V-2s, then with more powerful rockets that von Braun developed. Von Braun played an important part in making America's inter-continental ballistic missile, but the project closest to his heart was spaceflight. He was influential in the establishment of the US space agency, NASA. Von Braun's greatest achievement was the massive Saturn V rocket, the largest rocket ever built, which was used in the Apollo flights to the moon, and without which the "great leap for mankind" made by astronaut Neil Armstrong, the first man on the moon, would not have been possible.

(Top left) Von Braun (right) at Cape Kennedy (now Cape Canaveral). The Saturn V launch tower is in the background.

(Top right) The most powerful rocket ever built: a Saturn V lifts off with Apollo 15 on the way to the Moon, 1971.

(Left) A V-2 rocket bomb.

(Above) The V-bombs carried a large amount of explosive, and could cause extensive damage. Shown is the result of a hit on a hospital in Chelsea.

INDEX

CREDITS